50 STEP-BY-STEP HOME-MADE
PRESERVES

50 STEP-BY-STEP HOME-MADE PRESERVES

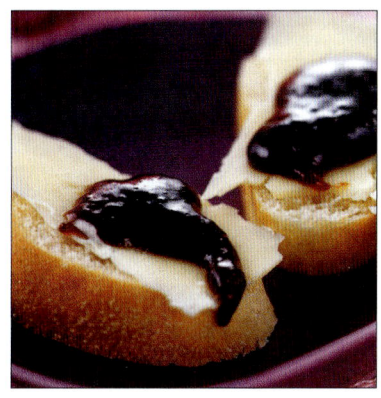

DELICIOUS EASY-TO-FOLLOW RECIPES FOR JAMS, JELLIES
AND SWEET CONSERVES, WITH 240 PHOTOGRAPHS

MAGGIE MAYHEW

This edition is published by Hermes House,
an imprint of Anness Publishing Ltd,
Hermes House, 88–89 Blackfriars Road, London SE1 8HA;
tel. 020 7401 2077; fax 020 7633 9499

www.hermeshouse.com; www.annesspublishing.com

If you like the images in this book and would like to investigate using them
for publishing, promotions or advertising, please visit our website
www.practicalpictures.com for more information.

© Anness Publishing Ltd 2008, 2010

All rights reserved. No part of this publication may be reproduced, stored
in a retrieval system, or transmitted in any way or by any means,
electronic, mechanical, photocopying, recording or otherwise,
without the prior written permission of the copyright holder.

Publisher: Joanna Lorenz
Editorial Director: Helen Sudell
Editors: Susannah Blake, Jennifer Mussett and Elizabeth Woodland
Photographer: Craig Robertson
Home Economist: Sarah O'Brien
Stylist: Helen Trent
Production Controller: Claire Rae

Previously published as part of a larger volume, *Preserves & Pickles*.

Main cover image shows Pink Grapefruit and Cranberry Marmalade –
for recipe, see page 62

ETHICAL TRADING POLICY
Because of our ongoing ecological investment programme, you, as our
customer, can have the pleasure and reassurance of knowing that a tree is
being cultivated on your behalf to naturally replace the materials used to
make the book you are holding. For further information about
this scheme, go to www.annesspublishing.com/trees

NOTES
Bracketed terms are intended for American readers.
Medium (US large) eggs are used unless otherwise stated.
For all recipes, quantities are given in both metric and imperial
measures and, where appropriate, measures are also given in standard
cups and spoons. Follow one set, but not a mixture, because they
are not interchangeable.
Standard spoon and cup measures are level.
1 tsp = 5ml, 1 tbsp = 15ml, 1 cup = 250ml/8fl oz
Australian standard tablespoons are 20ml. Australian readers
should use 3 tsp in place of 1 tbsp for measuring small quantities.

PUBLISHER'S NOTE
Although the advice and information in this book are believed to be accurate
and true at the time of going to press, neither the authors nor the publisher
can accept any legal responsibility or liability for any errors or omissions
that may be made nor for any inaccuracies nor for any harm or injury
that comes about from following instructions or advice in this book.

Contents

INTRODUCTION	6
EQUIPMENT	8
POTTING AND COVERING PRESERVES	10
MAKING JAMS, JELLIES AND MARMALADES	12
MAKING FRUIT CURDS, BUTTERS AND CHEESES	22
MAKING BOTTLED FRUITS	24
MAKING CANDIED AND GLACÉ FRUIT	26
MAKING DRIED FRUITS AND VEGETABLES	28
PRESERVING FRUITS IN ALCOHOL	29
MODERN PRESERVING TECHNIQUES	30
JAMS AND CONSERVES	**32**
SWEET FRUIT JELLIES	**44**
MARMALADES	**58**
CURDS, BUTTERS AND CHEESES	**70**
SWEET FRUIT PRESERVES	**84**
INDEX	96

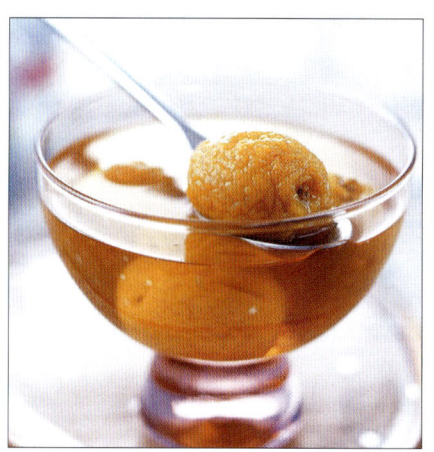

INTRODUCTION

Preserving seasonal fruits as jams and jellies is one of the oldest of culinary arts. Once essential for basic survival, preserving is nowadays more often employed for the wealth of rich flavours it can bring to every meal or snack. It can be done in two ways: by heat sterilization, which destroys enzymes and bacteria, or by creating an environment where contaminants are unable to thrive – by drying or by adding sugar, salt, vinegar or alcohol.

AN AGE-OLD TECHNIQUE

Preserving was one of the earliest skills acquired by man, essential for survival during the cold, dark winter months when fresh food was scarce. Sun and wind were the first natural agents to be used: fruits and vegetables laid out in the hot sun or hung in the wind to dry were found to last longer than fresh produce and were lighter and easier to carry. In colder, damp climates, smoke and fire were used to hasten the drying process.

These discoveries meant that travelling to new territories became easier and new settlements were built where it was feasible for people to both grow and store food. It wasn't long before early man found that salt was a powerful dehydrator, far more consistent and reliable than the natural elements of sun and wind. The preservative properties of vinegar and alcohol were discovered around the same time, and people also realized that food could be flavoured at the same time that it was being preserved.

Surprisingly the use of sugar as a preservative wasn't discovered until many centuries later. Cane sugar, brought to Europe by Arab merchants in the 12th century, remained a scarce luxury in the Western world for 400 years. It wasn't until the 16th century, when it was introduced to Europe from the West Indies, that sugar became a sought-after ingredient. Soon the demand for it became so great that it encouraged the rise of colonialism and the slave trade. In the 18th century, beetroot (beet), which had always been enjoyed as a vegetable, began to be cultivated specifically for its sugar content. Eventually sugar became plentiful and cheap, and the liking for sweet preserves started to grow.

It was during the 19th century that preserving really came into its own and was considered to be a skilled craft adopted in most households. Many of the recipes we use today are based on those that first appeared in cookbooks during that era. Housewives took pride in filling capacious pantries with an array of bottles and jars of sweet preserves, jams, jellies and marmalades. Most of these were made during the summer and autumn when berries and fruits were fresh and plentiful. These were then enjoyed during the lean winter months to supplement the diet, which would otherwise have consisted mainly of salted meats and root vegetables.

In the 20th century, preserving became less fashionable. Many homes had less storage space and, as the range and use of commercially prepared foods and preserves increased, huge stocks of home-made preserves were no longer needed or desirable.

Left: Rich, fruity jams have been a traditional method for preserving fruit for many centuries.

Above: Placing fruits in flavoured syrups was one of the earliest ways that sugar was used for preserving.

Imported produce meant that many fruits were available all year round – soft fruits could be bought in the winter months and citrus fruits never disappeared from grocers' shelves. By the middle of the century, refrigerators could be found in most homes, followed by freezers in the 1960s and 70s, and during those decades freezing became the preferred way of preserving fruit and vegetables and the old-fashioned techniques became less popular.

PRESERVE-MAKING TODAY

Nowadays, the art of preserving is coming back into its own, not because food needs to be processed to make it keep for long periods but for reasons of quality and variety. Improved travel and communication have increased knowledge of preserves from around the world and more unusual varieties of

Right: Nowadays fruit-packed home-made jams and conserves have become culinary treats.

fruit and flavouring ingredients are now readily available. Many people prefer to make their own preserves instead of buying mass-produced products with artificial flavourings and colourings. The satisfaction that comes from being able to create a unique product – especially when you have grown or picked your own fruit – is also being rediscovered. In some parts of the world it has become a flourishing cottage industry, with villages and towns becoming renowned for the quality of jams and other preserves, often focusing on locally grown or gathered fruits. The ease with which jams and preserves can be made in the home with simple equipment and ingredients makes jam-making a practical and enjoyable occupation for many in rural and urban environments alike.

This book contains a comprehensive and detailed reference section showing how to make jams, curds, butters and other sweet preserves. All the main techniques are shown, including jam-, jelly- and marmalade-making; bottling fruits; candying; drying; and preserving fruits in alcohol.

The stunning recipe collection includes a whole host of traditional and contemporary ideas that will prove to be an inspiration and pleasure to both the novice jam-maker and the experienced preserver.

EQUIPMENT

While very few specialist items are essential for preserving, having the correct equipment for the job will make the whole process easier and helps to ensure success. You will probably have most of the basic items such as a large heavy pan, weighing scales or calibrated measuring cups, wooden spoons, a chopping board and a few sharp knives. However, a few specific items such as a jam funnel for potting preserves and a jelly bag for straining fruit juices will prove invaluable. The following is a brief outline of the more useful items, all of which are readily available from large department stores and specialist kitchen equipment stores.

PRESERVING PAN

A preserving pan or large, heavy pan is essential. It must be of a sufficient size to allow rapid boiling without bubbling over (a capacity of about 9 litres/ 16 pints/8 quarts is ideal); wide enough to allow rapid evaporation of liquid, so that setting point is reached quickly; and have a thick heavy base to protect the preserve from burning. Preserving pans are fitted with a pair of short-looped handles, or a carrying handle over the top. A non-corrosive preserving pan such as one made of stainless steel is the best choice for making all types of preserves, and they are also readily available and inexpensive. Traditional copper preserving pans, usually very wide at the top and sloping to a narrow base, are intended only for jam- and jelly-making and are unsuitable for preserves containing lemon juice, or for acidic or red fruit, as both the flavour and colour will be spoilt. Enamel pans are not ideal as they do not conduct heat fast enough for preserving and they burn easily.

SUGAR THERMOMETER

Invaluable for cooking preserves to the exact temperature needed for a perfect set. Choose a thermometer that goes up to at least 110°C/ 230°F, and has a clip or a handle that can be attached to the pan, so that it does not slip into the boiling preserve.

JELLY BAG

Used to strain fruit juices from cooked fruit pulp for jelly-making, jelly bags are made from calico, cotton flannel or nylon. The close weave allows only the fruit juice to flow through, leaving the pulp behind. Some jelly bags have their own stands; others have loops with which to suspend the bag.

MUSLIN/CHEESECLOTH

Used for making spice and herb bags, muslin is also useful for tying together pips and peel, particularly when making marmalade. It can also be used instead of a jelly bag. To do this, layer three or four squares of muslin together and tie lengths of strong string (twine) securely to each corner. Either knot the ends together to hang from a single support, or make four loops so the bag can be suspended on the legs of an upturned stool or chair. Alternatively, line a large strainer with the muslin squares and place over a bowl to catch the juices.

JARS AND BOTTLES

When making preserves, a selection of containers is needed. Clear glass is ideal because it is non-corrosive, you can easily check for trapped air bubbles when potting preserves, and it looks very pretty when filled. As well as ordinary jam jars and bottles, there are specialist preserving jars that are designed to be heated to a high temperature. Non-corrosive seals are essential, particularly when potting more acidic preserves.

Be sure to choose appropriately shaped and sized containers. Wide-necked jars are essential for recipes using whole or large pieces of fruit, but for most preserves it is better to use several smaller jars than one or two large ones.

Left: A jelly bag with its own stand can make an easy job of straining jellies.

Preserves stored in very large jars are likely to deteriorate more quickly once the seal is broken; the preserve is not consumed as quickly and the contents are exposed to the air for longer than a preserve stored in a small jar.

PRESERVE COVERS

The cheapest way to cover jams, jellies and marmalades is to use a waxed paper disc and cellophane cover, secured by a rubber band; these covers are available to fit 450g/1lb and 900g/2lb jars. They are very easy to handle and use: simply lay the wax disc over the jam, jelly or marmalade in the jar and then secure the cellophane cover over the entire top of the jar with a rubber band, making it airtight.

HYDROMETER

Also known as a *pèse syrop*, a hydrometer measures the density of sugar syrup and is sometimes used when bottling fruit and for jam- and jelly-making. The tube is marked from 0 to 40 and measures the point to which the weighted tube sinks. The more sugar a syrup contains, the higher the hydrometer will float in it.

FUNNELS

These make potting preserves considerably easier. A jam funnel with a wide tube (10–13cm/4–5in diameter) that fits into the top of the jar or container can make quick, clean work of filling jars.

An ordinary funnel with a slimmer tube is useful for adding liquid to jars of fruit as well as for bottling smooth sauces and jellies. Some funnels have inner attachments that allow you to filter or strain the liquid while you are pouring. This can be useful for catching small pieces, although a proper strainer would be needed for more heavy filtering. Choose funnels made of heatproof plastic or stainless steel.

Above: A jam funnel can prove to be a real time-saver when potting jellies, jams and conserves.

Below: A selection of jars with either clamp-top, screw-top or two-piece screw-band lids are perfect for preserving.

POTTING AND COVERING PRESERVES

Make sure you have enough jars and bottles, and the correct sterilizing equipment, before you start to make any preserve.

CHOOSING CONTAINERS

To make the most of preserves, always pot them in the right type of container. It is better to pack preserves into several smaller containers rather than one large one, especially those that need to be consumed soon after opening.

Screw-top lidded jars are suitable for most sweet preserves. Clamp-top jars are also good as they produce an airtight vacuum that improves storage.

STERILIZING JARS AND BOTTLES

Before potting, it is essential to sterilize jars and bottles to destroy any micro-organisms in containers. Check jars and bottles for cracks or damage, then wash thoroughly in hot, soapy water, rinse well and turn upside-down to drain. Jars and bottles may be sterilized in five different ways: by heating in a low oven, immersing in boiling water, heating in a microwave, hot-washing in a dishwasher, or using sterilizing tablets.

oven method

Stand the containers, spaced slightly apart, on a baking sheet lined with kitchen paper. Rest any lids on top. Place in a cold oven, then heat to 110°C/225°F/Gas ¼ and bake for 30 minutes. Leave to cool slightly before filling. (If the jars or bottles are not used immediately, cover with a clean cloth and warm again before use.)

Below: Medium, wide-necked jars with plastic-coated screw-top lids are ideal for most preserves.

dishwasher method

This is the simplest way to clean and sterilize a large number of containers at the same time. Put the containers and lids in a dishwasher and run it on its hottest setting, including drying. If the jars are already washed and clean, you can run the cycle without adding detergent.

boiling water method

1 Place the containers, open-end up, in a deep pan that is wide enough to hold them in one layer.

2 Pour enough hot water into the pan to cover the containers. (Do not use boiling water because this can crack glass.) Bring the water to the boil and boil for 10 minutes.

3 Leave the containers in the pan until the water stops bubbling, then carefully remove and drain upside-down on a clean dishtowel. Turn the containers upright and leave to air-dry for a few minutes.

4 Immerse lids, seals and corks in simmering water for 20 seconds. (Only ever use corks once.)

STORAGE TIMES

Most preserves will keep for a year if packed and stored properly. Once opened, they should be eaten within 3 months. Some preserves have a shorter shelf-life:

Fruit curds, butters and cheeses can be stored in the refrigerator for 2–3 months and, once opened, should be used within 4 weeks.

Low-sugar jams and similar specialist preserves rely on sterilizing for their keeping qualities. They are usually processed commercially. Home-made versions are made in small quantities for short keeping in the refrigerator.

microwave method

This method is particularly useful when sterilizing only a few jars for potting a small amount of preserve. It is also quick and easy, so it is a useful method to use if you have limited time. Follow the microwave manufacturer's instructions and only use for jars that hold less than 450g/1lb and short squat bottles.

1 Half fill the clean jars or bottles with water and heat on full power until the water has boiled for at least 1 minute.

2 Using oven gloves, remove the jars or bottles from the microwave. Carefully swirl the water inside them, then pour it away. Drain upside-down on a clean dishtowel, then turn upright and leave to dry.

sterilizing tablet method

This easy-to-use method is not suitable for delicately flavoured preserves because the tablets may leave a slight taste. However, it is fine for robustly flavoured preserves. Following the instructions on the packet, dissolve the tablets and soak the containers in the sterilizing solution. Drain and dry thoroughly before use.

FILLING JARS

Most preserves should be potted into hot containers as soon as they are ready. Whole fruit jams, marmalades with peel, and jellies with added ingredients such as fresh herbs should be left to cool for 10 minutes until a thin skin forms on the surface. The preserve should then be stirred to distribute the ingredients and prevent them sinking once potted.

Different types of preserves need to be covered and sealed in different ways. Jams, conserves, jellies, marmalades and fruit cheeses can be covered with a waxed paper disc and the jar covered with cellophane held in place with a rubber band. Or the jar can be sealed with a screw-top lid. (Waxed discs and cellophane covers should not be used together with a screw-top lid.)

Bottled fruits must be sealed in jars with new rubber seals and vacuum or clamp-top lids. The latter are easy to use and very effective for keeping air out. They are readily available, although more costly than regular jars.

using waxed discs and cellophane covers

1 Using a heat-resistant ladle or jug (pitcher) and a jam funnel, carefully fill the jars with hot jam, almost to the top. Leave a small space of no more than 1cm/½in.

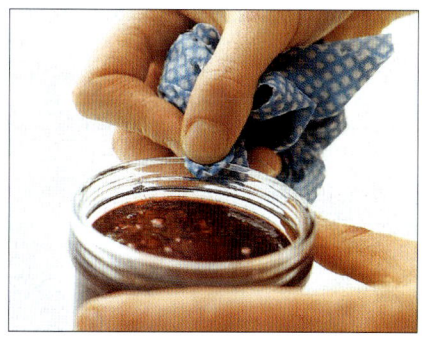

2 Using a clean, damp cloth, wipe the rim of the jar, making sure there are no dribbles of jam.

3 Place a waxed paper disc (waxed side down) on top of the preserve and smooth it down to form a good fit over the hot preserve.

4 Moisten a cellophane disc with a damp cloth and place on the jar, moist side up, then secure with an elastic band. Do this either when the preserve is very hot, or leave it to cool completely. (If sealed while warm, mould will grow on the surface.) As it dries, the cellophane will shrink, creating a tight seal.

potting and covering preserves • 11

MAKING JAMS, JELLIES AND MARMALADES

These are made from fruit boiled with sugar until setting point is reached. They rely on pectin, sugar and acid for a good set. Pectin is a natural, gum-like substance, which is essential in jam-, jelly- and marmalade-making. Found in the cores, pips (seeds), pith and skins of fruits, it reacts with sugar and acid to form the gel that helps to set jams, jellies and marmalades.

testing pectin content

Pectin content can vary according to the variety of fruit, when it is picked, and growing conditions. It is best to test for pectin content at an early stage in jam-making, and add extra pectin if necessary.

1 To test for pectin content, cook the fruit until soft, then spoon 5ml/1 tsp of the juices into a glass. Add 15ml/1 tbsp methylated spirits (denatured alcohol) and shake.

2 After 1 minute a clot should form: one large jelly-like clot indicates high pectin content; two or three small clots indicate the pectin content is medium and should achieve a set; lots of small clots, or no clots at all indicate low pectin content and that extra pectin will be needed for a set.

3 If the pectin content is medium, add 15ml/1 tbsp lemon juice for every 450g/1lb fruit. If the pectin content is low, add 75–90ml/ 5–6 tbsp pectin stock for every 450g/1lb fruit. Alternatively, add pectin powder or liquid, or use sugar containing pectin.

making pectin stock

Home-made pectin stock is very easy to make and can be stirred into low-pectin fruit jams and jellies to improve their set. Stir in after the initial cooking of the fruit and before the sugar is added. A teaspoon of the juices can be taken from the pan at this stage and tested for pectin content.

1 Roughly chop 900g/2lb cooking apples, including the cores, peel and pips. Place in a large heavy pan and pour over cold water to cover. Bring to the boil, then reduce the heat, cover and simmer for 40 minutes, or until very soft.

2 Pour the mixture into a sterilized jelly bag suspended over a bowl. Leave to drain for at least 2 hours.

3 Pour the drained juices into the cleaned pan and boil for about 20 minutes, or until the volume is reduced by one-third.

4 Pour the pectin stock into 150ml/¼ pint/⅔ cup sterilized containers and store in the refrigerator for up to 1 week or freeze for up to 4 months.

5 To use frozen pectin stock, defrost at room temperature, or overnight in the refrigerator, then stir into the preserve.

TESTING FOR A SET
Some preserves reach setting point quickly, so check early in the cooking time.

Wrinkle test Remove the preserve from the heat and spoon a little preserve on to a chilled plate. Leave to cool for 1 minute, then push the preserve with a finger; the top should wrinkle. If it wrinkles only slightly, return the preserve to the heat and cook for 2 minutes more, then test again.

Flake test Coat a spoon in the preserve; cool for a few seconds, then hold the spoon horizontally. When shaken, the jam should run off the side in one flat flake.

Thermometer test Briefly stir the preserve, dip a jam thermometer into very hot water, then place in the preserve. Move it around, but do not touch the pan base. Jams and marmalades reach setting point at 105°C/220°F; jellies and conserves a degree lower.

MAKING JAM

Usually made with whole or cut fruit, jam should have distinct flavour, bright colour and soft set.

making summer fruit jam

Use sound, slightly under-ripe fruit; over-ripe fruit contains less pectin and will not set well.

Makes about 1.6kg/3½lb

INGREDIENTS

900g/2lb mixed fruits, such as cherries, raspberries, strawberries, gooseberries, blackcurrants and redcurrants

2.5–20ml/½–4 tsp lemon juice

900g/2lb/4½ cups preserving or granulated sugar

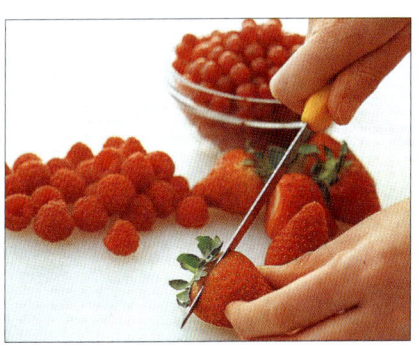

1 Weigh each type of fruit, then prepare. Rinse and drain cherries, gooseberries, blackcurrants and redcurrants; wash raspberries and strawberries only if necessary; remove any stems and leaves and cut off any damaged parts.

2 Put the lemon juice in a large heavy pan: strawberries and cherries are low in pectin, so add 10ml/2 tsp lemon juice for each 450g/1lb fruit; add 2.5ml/½ tsp for each 450g/1lb raspberries; and add no lemon juice for high-pectin gooseberries and currants.

3 Put the prepared gooseberries, blackcurrants and redcurrants in the pan with 60ml/4 tbsp water and cook over a low heat for 5 minutes until the skins soften.

4 Add the raspberries, cherries and strawberries to the pan. (If using only these fruits, do not add any water.) Cook for 10 minutes until all the fruit is just tender.

5 Using the back of a spoon, crush one-third of the fruit to release the pectin. If using a high proportion of strawberries or cherries, do a pectin test at this stage.

6 Add the sugar to the pan and stir over a low heat until it has dissolved completely. Increase the heat and bring to the boil. Continue to boil rapidly for about 10 minutes, stirring occasionally, until setting point is reached (105°C/220°F). Skim off any froth that rises to the surface.

IS IT A JAM, CONSERVE OR SPREAD?

Understanding the labels on store-bought preserves can be difficult. Here's a brief guide:

Jam This contains a minimum of 30g/1¼oz fruit and 60g/2¼oz/generous ¼ cup sugar per 100g/3¾oz jam. It may contain colourings, preservatives and gelling agents.

Extra jam This must contain at least 45g/1¾oz whole fruit per 100g/3¾oz jam. It contains no colourings, preservatives or flavourings.

Reduced-sugar jam This has a minimum of 35g/1½oz fruit and 30–55g/1¼–2¼oz sugar per 100g/3¾oz jam.

Conserve This implies a quality jam with a high fruit content, but check the label. Usually, the fruit is whole and steeped in sugar before cooking, giving a softer set.

Fruit spreads These are made from fruit pulps sweetened with fruit juice.

7 Remove the pan from the heat and leave to stand for 5 minutes. If necessary, skim off any froth, then stir to distribute larger pieces of fruit. Pot, seal and label.

making jams, jellies and marmalades • 13

making seedless raspberry jam

Some fruits, notably raspberries and blackberries, contain a large number of pips (seeds), which result in a very "pippy" jam or conserve. If you prefer a smooth jam without pips, they can be removed after initial cooking by pressing the fruit through a nylon or stainless steel sieve (strainer).

Makes about 750g/1⅔lb

INGREDIENTS

450g/1lb/2⅔ cups raspberries
about 450g/1lb/2¼ cups preserving or granulated sugar

1 Use a mixture of just-ripe and a few slightly underripe berries to ensure a good set. Put the fruit in a large heavy pan and gently crush to release the juices using the back of a wooden spoon.

2 Gently heat the fruit mixture to boiling point, then simmer for about 10 minutes, stirring now and then, until the fruit is really soft.

3 Pour the mixture into a fine nylon or stainless steel sieve placed over a bowl and push through the fruit purée using the back of the wooden spoon. Discard the pips left in the sieve.

4 Measure the fruit pulp into the cleaned pan, adding 450g/1lb/2¼ cups sugar for each 600ml/1 pint/2½ cups purée. Heat gently, stirring, until the sugar dissolves, then boil rapidly until setting point is reached (105°C/220°F).

5 Using a slotted spoon, skim any froth from the surface, then pot the jam, cover and seal.

making cherry jam with commercial pectin

Fruits with a low pectin content require additional pectin to achieve a good set. Adding commercial pectin is an easy way to do this. Jams made in this way need only short boiling and require little or no water and a smaller proportion of fruit to sugar.

Makes about 1.8kg/4lb

INGREDIENTS

1.2kg/2½lb/6 cups pitted cherries
150ml/¼ pint/⅔ cup water
45ml/3 tbsp lemon juice
1.3kg/3lb/generous 6¼ cups granulated sugar
250ml/8fl oz/1 cup liquid pectin

1 Put the cherries, water and lemon juice in a large pan. Cover and cook for 15 minutes, stirring, until the cherries are tender.

2 Add the sugar to the pan and stir over a low heat until dissolved completely. Bring to the boil and boil rapidly for 1 minute.

3 Stir the liquid pectin into the jam, return to the boil and cook for 1 minute.

4 Remove the pan from the heat and, using a slotted spoon, skim off any froth from the surface. Set the jam aside and leave to stand for 5 minutes.

5 Stir the jam briefly to distribute the fruit evenly, then pot and seal. Use within 6 months.

PECTIN CONTENT OF FRUIT

Although the pectin content of fruits can vary depending on variety, growing conditions and when the fruits were picked, the list below can be used as a good basic guide to the set that will be achieved.

High Apples, blackcurrants, cranberries, damsons, gooseberries, grapefruit, lemons, limes, loganberries, redcurrants, quinces

Medium Apricots (fresh), apples (eating), bilberries, blackberries (early), grapes, greengages, mulberries, peaches, plums, raspberries

Low Bananas, blackberries (late), cherries, elderberries, figs, guavas, japonica, melons, nectarines, pears, pineapples, rhubarb, strawberries

MAKING CONSERVES

These are very similar to jams, but they have a slightly softer set and contain whole or large pieces of fruit. The fruit is first mixed with sugar and sometimes a little liquid, then allowed to stand for several hours or even days. The sugar draws out the juices from the fruit, making it firmer and minimizing the cooking time needed. The fruit should be just ripe and even in size. Not all fruit is suitable for making conserves; tough fruit skins do not soften when sugar is added, so fruits such as gooseberries are no good for making conserves.

making strawberry conserve

This preserve takes several days to make, so be sure to leave plenty of time for preparation.

Makes about 1.3kg/3lb

INGREDIENTS
1.3kg/3lb small or medium strawberries, hulled
1.3kg/3lb/generous 6¾ cups granulated sugar

1 Layer the hulled strawberries in a large bowl with the sugar. Cover with clear film (plastic wrap) and chill for 24 hours.

2 Transfer the strawberries, sugar and juices to a large heavy pan. Heat gently, stirring occasionally, until the sugar has dissolved. Bring to the boil and cook steadily (not rapidly) for 5 minutes.

3 Leave the mixture to cool, then place in a bowl, cover with clear film and chill for 2 days.

4 Pour the strawberry mixture into a large pan, bring to the boil and cook steadily for 10 minutes, then remove from the heat and set aside for 10 minutes. Stir, then ladle into warmed sterilized jars and seal.

flavouring conserves

Conserves are more luxurious than jams and often include dried fruit, nuts and spirits or liqueurs. These extra ingredients should be added after setting point is reached.

When adding dried fruit or nuts, chop them evenly and allow about 50g/2oz/½ cup fruit or nuts per 750g/1⅔lb conserve.

Choose spirits or liqueurs that complement the flavour of the chosen fruit. For example, add apricot brandy or amaretto liqueur to apricot conserve, kirsch to cherry conserve and ginger wine to melon conserve; allow 30ml/2 tbsp to every 750g/1⅔lb conserve.

TOP TIPS FOR SUCCESSFUL JAM-MAKING

• Always use the freshest fruit possible and avoid overripe fruit.

• If you wash the fruit, dry it well and use promptly because it will deteriorate on standing.

• Cook the fruit very slowly at first over a low heat to extract the maximum amount of juice and pectin. Stir the fruit frequently until very tender, but do not overcook. (Fruit skins toughen once sugar is added.)

• Warm the sugar in a low oven for about 10 minutes before adding it to the fruit. This will help it to dissolve.

• Stir the preserve to ensure the sugar is completely dissolved before boiling.

• Do not stir frequently when boiling. This lowers the temperature and delays reaching setting point.

• It is wasteful to remove scum too often. To help prevent scum from forming, add a small amount of unsalted (sweet) butter (about 15g/½oz/1 tbsp for every 450g/1lb fruit) when you add the sugar.

• Do not move freshly potted preserves until they are cool and have set completely.

MAKING JELLIES

Jellies are made using the juice strained from simmered fruit, which is then boiled with sugar to setting point. There is very little preparation of fruit, other than giving it a quick rinse and roughly chopping larger fruit, but you do need to allow plenty of time to make the jelly itself. The secret to a beautifully clear jelly lies in straining the fruit pulp through a jelly bag, drip by drip, which takes several hours.

The basic principles of jelly-making are the same as those for jam and the same three substances – pectin, sugar and acid – are needed for the jelly to set. A perfectly set jelly should retain its shape and quiver when spooned out of the jar. Fruits that are low in pectin such as strawberries, cherries and pears are not suitable on their own for making jellies, so are usually combined with high-pectin fruit.

Because the fruit pulp is discarded in jelly-making, the yield is not as large as in jam-making. For this reason many jelly recipes have evolved to make the most of wild fruits, which are free, or gluts of home-grown fruit.

Jellies can be served both as sweet and savoury preserves. Some, such as redcurrant, rowan and cranberry jellies, are classic accompaniments for hot or cold roasted meat or game, or are added to gravy for flavour and give an attractive glossy finish. Savoury jellies often contain chopped herbs and sometimes wine vinegar or cider vinegar to give them a sharper flavour. Sweet jellies may be eaten as a spread.

yield of jelly

The final yield of jelly depends on how juicy the fruit is, and this can vary depending on the time of the year, the weather during growth and its ripeness when harvested. Because of this, the juice, rather than the fruit, is measured and the amount of sugar is calculated accordingly. As a general rule, 450g/1lb/2¼ cups sugar is added for each 600ml/1 pint/2½ cups juice. (If the fruit is very rich in pectin, the recipe may suggest adding slightly less sugar.) As a rough guide, recipes containing 450g/1lb/2¼ cups sugar will make about 675–800g/1½–1¾lb jelly.

making redcurrant jelly

Makes about 1.3kg/3lb

INGREDIENTS

1.3kg/3lb just-ripe redcurrants
600ml/1 pint/2½ cups water
about 900g/2lb/4½ cups preserving or granulated sugar

1 Check the fruit is clean. If necessary, rinse in cold water and use a little less water in the recipe.

2 Remove the currants from the stalks. There is no need to top and tail the fruit.

3 Place the redcurrants in a large heavy pan with the water and simmer gently for about 30 minutes, or until the fruit is very soft and pulpy. Stir occasionally during cooking to prevent the fruit from catching and burning.

4 Pour the cooked fruit and juices into a sterilized jelly bag suspended over a large bowl. Leave to drain for about 4 hours, or until the juice stops dripping. (Do not press or squeeze the fruit in the bag because this will result in a cloudy jelly.)

5 Discard the pulp remaining in the bag (unless you plan to boil the pulp a second time – see page 34). Pour the juice into the cleaned pan and add 450g/1lb/2¼ cups warmed sugar for each 600ml/1 pint/2½ cups of juice. (When making jellies with low-pectin fruit, stir in a little lemon juice or vinegar to improve the set. This will also help to offset the sweetness of the jelly.)

6 Heat the mixture gently, stirring frequently, until the sugar has completely dissolved, then increase the heat and bring to the boil.

7 Boil the jelly rapidly for about 10 minutes, or until setting point is reached. You can check this using the flake test or wrinkle test, or you can use a jam thermometer. The jelly should be heated to 105°C/220°F.

8 Remove the pan from the heat, then skim any froth from the surface of the jelly using a slotted spoon.

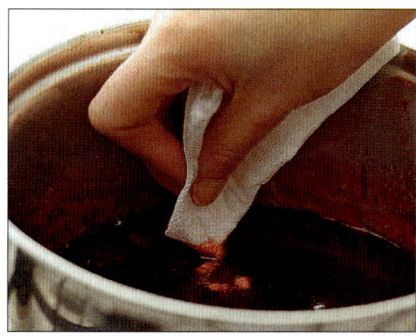

9 Carefully remove the last traces of froth using a piece of kitchen paper. Pot the jelly immediately because it will start to set fairly quickly.

10 Cover and seal the jelly while it is hot, then leave to cool completely. (Do not move or tilt the jars until the jelly is completely cold and set.) Label the jars and store in a cool, dark place.

USING A JELLY BAG

Jelly bags, which are made from heavy-duty calico, cotton flannel or close-weave nylon, allow only the juice from the fruit to flow through, leaving the skins, pulp and pips (seeds) inside the bag. The fruit pulp and juices are very heavy, so strong tape or loops are positioned on the corners for hanging the bag securely on a stand, upturned stool or chair.

1 Before use, sterilize the jelly bag by scalding in boiling water. This process also helps the juices to run through the bag, rather than being absorbed into it.

2 If you don't have a jelly bag, you can use three or four layers of sterilized muslin (cheesecloth) or a piece of fine linen cloth instead. Simply line a large nylon or stainless-steel sieve (strainer) with the muslin or linen.

3 Carefully suspend the jelly bag or lined sieve over a large bowl to catch the juice. Make sure the bag or sieve is secure before spooning some of the simmered fruit and juices into it. (Don't add too much to start with.)

4 Leave the fruit to drain for a while, then spoon in more fruit. Continue gradually adding fruit in this way until it has all been placed in the bag or sieve, then leave to drain until it stops dripping completely. Some fruits will take 2–3 hours to release all their juice, while others may take as long as 12 hours.

5 Immediately after use, wash the jelly bag thoroughly, then rinse several times to remove all traces of detergent. Ensure the bag is completely dry before storing. The jelly bag may be reused many times, but be sure to sterilize it before every use.

making jams, jellies and marmalades • 17

boiling fruit twice

Rather than discarding the fruit pulp from the jelly bag after draining, you can boil it again to extract more liquid and flavour. This should be done only with pectin-rich fruits such as sharp apples, damsons or currants. The resulting jelly may have a slightly less concentrated flavour than jelly made from juice obtained from fruit that has been boiled once.

To boil the fruit a second time, return the fruit pulp to the pan and add just enough cold water to cover, using no more than half the amount of water used for the first boiling. Simmer the fruit gently for about 20 minutes, then drain through the jelly bag as before. Add the juice to the first batch.

flavouring jelly

Jellies are sometimes flavoured with fresh herbs and flowers such as mint, rosemary and geranium leaves. In some the herb is most important and the fruit provides a base in which to suspend the herb; in others, herbs are used in small quantities to impart a subtle flavour.

1 To simply add flavour, add sprigs of herbs at the beginning of cooking. Woody herbs should be removed before straining because stems may damage the jelly bag.

2 When adding finely chopped herbs to the finished jelly, even distribution can be difficult and, if the jelly is too hot, the pieces may float to the top. To overcome this problem, put the herbs in a sieve (strainer) and sprinkle with a little water to dampen them.

3 Leave the jelly to stand until it just starts to form a thin skin on top, then quickly stir in the chopped herbs. Pot straight away in very warm, but not hot, sterilized jars and seal. Cool before labelling.

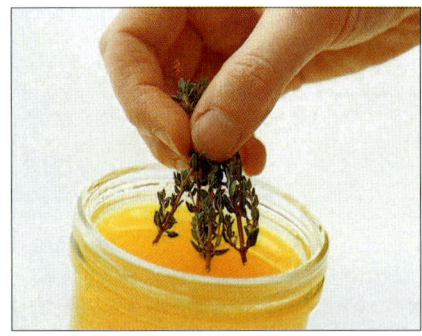

4 Herb sprigs and aromatic leaves, such as lemon verbena or geranium leaves, can look stunning set in jelly. Pour the jelly into sterilized jars, then leave until semi-set and insert the herb sprigs or leaves.

TOP TIPS FOR SUCCESSFUL JELLY-MAKING

• There is no need to peel or stone (pit) fruit before cooking because all the debris will be removed during straining. However, it is important to discard any bruised or mouldy parts of the fruit because these will spoil the flavour. Rinse the fruit only if dusty or dirty.

• If using fruits such as apples that require longer cooking, chop the fruit very finely to reduce the cooking time required. Cooking the fruit for a shorter time also helps to give the jelly an intense, fresh flavour.

• Simmer the fruit very gently to extract the maximum amount of pectin and to avoid evaporating too much liquid. When cooking hard fruits that take a long time to soften, cover the pan for the first half of the cooking time to reduce the amount of liquid lost.

• Some fruits, such as redcurrants or blackcurrants, can be cooked in the oven to make highly flavoured jellies. Place the fruit in an ovenproof dish with about 75ml/5 tbsp water, cover tightly and cook at 140°C/275°F/Gas 1 for about 50 minutes, stirring occasionally, until pulpy. Drain through a jelly bag, then add 425g/15oz/generous 2 cups sugar for every 600ml/ 1 pint/2½ cups strained juice.

• Jellies set very quickly, so pot immediately. Warm a stainless steel funnel in the oven, or rinse a plastic one under hot water and dry it, then use to pot the jelly. If the jelly starts to set in the pan, warm it briefly until liquid again.

• Gently tap the jars as you fill with jelly to remove air bubbles.

• Although you can add a little butter to jam to disperse any scum, do not do this with jelly – it will make it cloudy.

MAKING MARMALADES

This preserve consists of a jelly base, usually with small pieces of fruit suspended in it. The name marmalade is derived from the Portuguese word *marmelo*, meaning quince, and it was from this fruit that marmalades were first made.

Modern marmalades are usually made from citrus fruits, or citrus fruits combined with other fruits such as pineapple, or flavoured with aromatic spices. Marmalades can range from thick and dark to light and translucent.

The citrus peel is shredded and cooked with the fruit juices and water until soft and tender, then boiled with sugar to make the marmalade. Citrus peel requires long, slow cooking in a large amount of water to become soft. The pith of Seville oranges, lemons and grapefruits becomes clear when cooked, but that of sweet oranges does not, so the pith should be scraped off the rind before shredding and cooking.

As well as classic marmalade, there is also jelly marmalade. This is perfect for people who enjoy the flavour of marmalade but do not like the peel that is suspended in the jelly. Rather than adding the shredded rind to the juices and water in the pan, the rind is tied in a muslin (cheesecloth) bag to keep it separate. The juices are then strained and boiled to setting point. The jelly may be left plain and potted as it is, or a little of the shredded rind can be stirred into the jelly just before potting. As with any jelly, it is difficult to give an exact yield for jelly marmalade.

making seville orange marmalade

Bitter Seville oranges are very popular for marmalade-making.

Makes about 2.5kg/5½lb

INGREDIENTS
900g/2lb Seville oranges
1 large lemon
2.4 litres/4 pints/2 quarts water
1.8kg/4lb/generous 9 cups preserving or granulated sugar

1 Wash and dry the fruits. If you are using waxed oranges and lemons, scrub the skins gently.

2 Halve the fruits and squeeze out the juice and pips (seeds), then pour into a muslin- (cheesecloth-)lined sieve (strainer) set over a bowl.

3 Remove some of the pith from the citrus peels and reserve, then cut the peel into narrow strips.

4 Add the reserved pith to the pips in the muslin and tie together to make a loose bag. Allow plenty of room so that the water can bubble through the bag and extract the pectin from the pith and pips.

5 Place the shredded peel, juices and the muslin bag in a large preserving pan and pour in the water. Using a clean ruler, measure the depth of the contents in the pan and make a note of it.

6 Slowly bring the mixture to the boil and simmer for 1½–2 hours, or until the peel is very soft and the contents have reduced by about half their depth.

COOK'S TIPS

• To save time, shred the citrus peel in a food processor rather than by hand. Use either the fine or coarse cutting attachment.

• If you can't find Seville oranges, use Temple oranges instead.

making jams, jellies and marmalades • 19

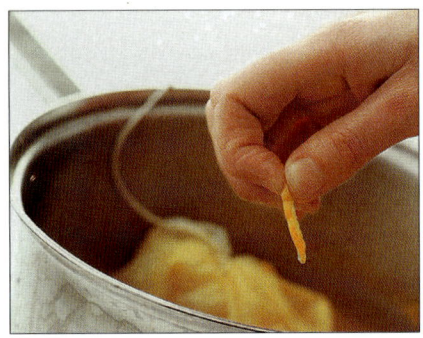

7 To check that the peel is cooked, remove a piece from the pan and leave for a few minutes to cool. Once cooled, press the peel between finger and thumb; it should feel very soft.

8 Using a slotted spoon, remove the muslin bag from the pan and set it aside until cool enough to handle. Squeeze as much liquid as possible back into the pan to extract all the pectin from the pips and pith.

9 Add the sugar to the pan and stir over a low heat until the sugar has completely dissolved.

10 Bring the marmalade to the boil, then boil rapidly for about 10 minutes until setting point is reached (105°C/220°F). You may also use the flake or wrinkle test to check the set.

11 Using a slotted spoon, remove any scum from the surface of the marmalade, then leave to cool until a thin skin starts to form on the surface of the preserve.

12 Leave the marmalade to stand for about 5 minutes, then stir gently to distribute the peel evenly. Ladle into hot sterilized jars, then cover and seal.

making orange jelly marmalade

This recipe uses Seville oranges, and may be made as a plain jelly marmalade, or a few fine shreds of peel can be added before potting, which can look very pretty and adds an interesting texture. Any marmalade can be made in the same way; use exactly the same ingredients listed in the recipe but use the method below.

Makes about 2kg/4½lb

INGREDIENTS

450g/1lb Seville (Temple) oranges
1.75 litres/3 pints/7½ cups water
1.3kg/3lb/generous 6¾ cups preserving or granulated sugar
60ml/4 tbsp lemon juice

1 Wash and dry the oranges; gently scrub them with a soft brush if they have waxed skins.

2 If you want to add a little peel to the jelly marmalade, thinly pare and finely shred the rind from 2 or 3 of the oranges. Place the shreds in a square of muslin (cheesecloth) and tie it into a neat bag.

3 Halve the oranges and squeeze out the juice and pips (seeds), then pour the juice and pips into a large preserving pan.

4 Roughly chop the orange peel, including all the pith, and add it to the pan. Add the bag of shredded rind, if using, and pour over the water. Cover the pan with a lid and leave to soak for at least 4 hours, or overnight.

5 Bring the mixture to the boil, then reduce the heat and simmer gently for 1½ hours. Using a slotted spoon, remove the bag of peel, and carefully remove a piece of peel to check that it is tender. If not, re-tie the bag and simmer for a further 15–20 minutes. Remove the bag of peel and set aside.

6 Line a large nylon or stainless steel sieve (strainer) with a double layer of muslin and place over a large bowl. Pour boiling water through the muslin to scald it. Discard the scalding water. Alternatively, use a scalded jelly bag suspended over a bowl instead of the muslin-lined sieve.

7 Pour the fruit and juices into the sieve or jelly bag and leave to drain for at least 1 hour. Pour the juices into the cleaned pan.

8 Add the sugar, lemon juice and shredded orange rind, if using, to the pan. Stir over a low heat until the sugar has dissolved, then bring to the boil and boil rapidly for about 10 minutes until setting point is reached (105°C/220°F).

9 Remove any scum from the surface. Leave to cool until a thin skin starts to form on the surface. Stir, then pot, cover and seal.

TOP TIPS FOR SUCCESSFUL MARMALADE-MAKING

• Always wash citrus fruit well. Most citrus fruits have a wax coating that helps to prolong the life of the fruit, which should be removed before making the fruit into marmalade. Alternatively, buy unwaxed fruit, but always rinse before use.

• When shredding peel, always slice it slightly thinner than required in the finished preserve because the rind will swell slightly during cooking.

• Coarse-cut peel will take longer to soften than finely shredded peel. To reduce cooking time, soak the peel for a few hours in the water and juices before cooking.

• If the fruit needs to be peeled, put it in a bowl of boiling water and leave to stand for a couple of minutes. This will help to loosen the skins and make peeling easier. The rind's flavour will leach into the water, so use the soaking water in place of some of the measured water.

• If using small, thin-skinned fruit such as limes, cut the fruit into quarters lengthways, then slice flesh and rind into thin or thick shreds. If using larger, thick-skinned fruit such as grapefruit, pare off the peel, including some white pith, and shred. Cut the fruit into quarters, remove the remaining white pith and roughly chop the flesh.

• To make a coarse-cut preserve, boil the whole fruit for 2 hours until soft; pierce with a skewer to test. Lift out the fruit, halve, prise out the pips, then tie them loosely in muslin (cheesecloth) and add to the hot water. Boil rapidly for 10 minutes, then remove the bag. Slice the fruit and return to the pan. Stir in the sugar until dissolved, then boil to setting point.

• Shredded peel should be simmered gently; fierce cooking can give a tough result. Check that the peel is really soft before adding the sugar because it will not tenderize further after this.

• For easy removal, tie the muslin bag of pith and pips with string and attach it to the pan handle. It can then be lifted out of the boiling mixture easily.

• If the fruit contains a lot of pith, put only a small amount in the muslin bag with the pips. Put the remaining pith in a small pan, cover with water and boil for 10 minutes. Strain the liquid and use in place of some of the measured water for the recipe.

• To flavour marmalade with liqueur or spirits, add 15–30ml/ 1–2 tbsp for every 450g/1lb/ 2¼ cups sugar – stir it in just before potting. Unsweetened apple juice or dry (hard) cider may be used to replace up to half the water to add flavour to marmalades made with sharper fruits such as kumquats.

making jams, jellies and marmalades • 21

MAKING FRUIT CURDS, BUTTERS AND CHEESES

These rich, creamy preserves were once the highlight of an English tea during Edwardian and Victorian times. Curds and butters are delicious spread on slices of fresh bread and butter, or used as fillings for cakes; firmer fruit cheeses are usually sliced and can be enjoyed in similar ways. Fruit cheeses and butters are also very good served with roast meat, game or cheese.

Curds are made from fruit juice or purée cooked with eggs and butter. They have a soft texture and short keeping qualities. Fruit butters and cheeses are made from fruit purée boiled with sugar and are good if you have a glut of fruit because they require a relatively high proportion of fruit. Butters are lower in sugar and cooked for a shorter time, producing a soft, fruity preserve with a short shelf-life. Cheeses have a firm texture and may be set in moulds and turned out to serve.

MAKING FRUIT CURDS

Fruit curds are usually made with the juice of citrus fruits, but other acidic fruits such as passion fruit may be used. Smooth purées made from, for example, cooking apples or gooseberries can also be used.

The juice or purée is heated with eggs, butter and sugar until thick. The mixture is always cooked in a double boiler or a bowl set over a pan of simmering water to prevent the eggs curdling. Whole eggs are generally used, but if there is a lot of juice, egg yolks or a combination of whole eggs and yolks give a thicker result.

making lime curd

Makes about 675g/1½lb

INGREDIENTS

5 large, ripe juicy limes
115g/4oz/½ cup butter, cubed, at room temperature
350g/12oz/scant 1¾ cups caster (superfine) sugar
4 eggs, at room temperature

1 Finely grate the lime rind, ensuring you do not include any of the bitter white pith. Halve the limes and squeeze out the juice.

2 Place the lime rind in a large heatproof bowl set over a pan of barely simmering water, then strain in the lime juice to remove any bits of fruit or pips (seeds).

3 Add the cubed butter and the sugar to the bowl. Heat gently, stirring frequently, until the butter melts; the mixture should be barely warm, not hot.

4 Lightly beat the eggs with a fork, then strain through a fine sieve into the warm fruit mixture.

5 Keeping the water at a very gentle simmer, stir the fruit mixture continuously until the curd is thick enough to coat the back of a wooden spoon. Do not overcook because the curd will thicken on cooling.

6 Spoon the curd into warmed sterilized jars, then cover and seal when cold. Store in a cool, dark place, ideally in the refrigerator. Use within 2 months.

MAKING FRUIT BUTTERS

Smoother and thicker than jam, fruit butters have a spreadable quality not unlike dairy butter. Many recipes also contain a small amount of butter.

making apricot butter

Makes about 1.3kg/3lb

INGREDIENTS

1.3kg/3lb fresh ripe apricots
1 large orange
about 450ml/¾ pint/scant 2 cups water
about 675g/1½lb/scant 3½ cups caster (superfine) sugar
15g/½oz/1 tbsp butter (optional)

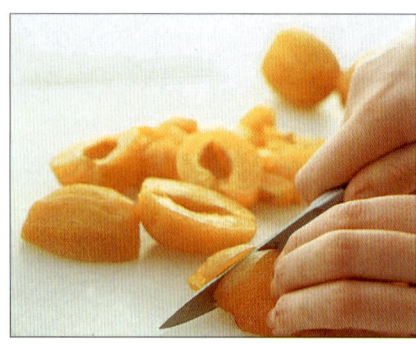

1 Rinse the apricots, then halve, stone (pit) and roughly chop. Remove the skins, unless you are going to purée the fruit by pressing through a sieve (strainer).

2 Scrub the orange and thinly pare 2–3 large strips of rind, avoiding any pith. Squeeze out the juice and put the apricots and the orange rind and juice in a large heavy pan.

3 Pour over enough of the water to cover the fruit. Bring to the boil, half-cover, then reduce the heat and simmer for 45 minutes.

4 Remove the orange rind, then blend the apricot mixture in a food processor until very smooth. Alternatively, press through a fine nylon or stainless steel sieve.

5 Measure the apricot purée and return it to the cleaned pan, adding 375g/13oz/1¾ cups sugar for each 600ml/1 pint/2½ cups purée.

6 Heat the mixture gently, stirring, until the sugar has dissolved, then bring to the boil and boil for about 20 minutes, stirring frequently, until thick and creamy. Remove the pan from the heat.

7 If using, stir the butter into the mixture until melted. (The butter gives a glossy finish.) Spoon into warmed sterilized jars and cover. Store in the refrigerator and use within 6 months.

MAKING FRUIT CHEESES

These sweet, firm preserves are known as cheeses because they are stiff enough to be cut into slices or wedges rather like their dairy counterparts. This name is particularly appropriate when the cheeses are set in moulds and turned out. They may be made either from fresh fruit, or from the pulp left from making jellies.

making cranberry and apple cheese

Makes about 900g/2lb

INGREDIENTS
450g/1lb/4 cups fresh cranberries
225g/8oz cooking apples
600ml/1 pint/2½ cups water
10ml/2 tsp lemon juice
about 450g/1lb/2¼ cups granulated sugar
glycerine, for greasing (optional)

1 Rinse the cranberries and place in a large heavy pan. Wash the apples and cut into small pieces (there is no need to peel or core). Add the water and lemon juice.

2 Cover the pan with a lid and bring the mixture to the boil; do not lift the lid until the cranberries stop popping because they often jump out of the pan and can be very hot. Simmer gently for 1 hour, or until the fruit is soft and pulpy.

3 Press the mixture through a fine nylon or stainless steel sieve (strainer) into a bowl.

4 Weigh the purée, then return it to the cleaned pan, adding 450g/1lb/ 2¼ cups sugar for every 450g/1lb purée. Gently heat the mixture over a low heat, stirring, until the sugar has dissolved completely.

5 Increase the heat a little and simmer the mixture until it is so thick that the spoon leaves a clean line through the mixture when drawn across the pan. It may take as long as 30 minutes to reduce the purée to this consistency. Stir frequently to stop the mixture burning on the base of the pan.

6 Spoon the fruit cheese into warmed sterilized jars and seal. Alternatively, spoon the mixture into moulds or jars greased with a little glycerine and cover with clear film (plastic wrap) when cool. In sealed jars, the cheese will keep for up to 1 year; in covered moulds, it should be kept in the refrigerator until you are ready to turn it out; eat within 1 month of making.

USING LEFTOVER PULP
The fruit pulp left from jelly-making is perfect for making into fruit cheeses. Remove the pulp from the jelly bag, stir in enough hot water to make a soft purée, then push through a sieve (strainer). Place the purée in a clean pan, adding 450g/1lb/2¼ cups sugar for every 450g/1lb purée, and follow the instructions for making fruit cheese above.

making fruit curds, butters and cheeses • 23

MAKING BOTTLED FRUITS

This is a traditional method of preserving fruit in syrup. The jars or bottles of fruit and syrup are heated to destroy micro-organisms. Although superseded by freezing, bottling is more suitable for some fruits such as peaches, pears, grapes and oranges; the method is less suitable for preserving soft berries such as raspberries.

making bottled fresh fruit salad

Makes about 1.8kg/4lb

INGREDIENTS
250g/9oz/generous 1¼ cups granulated sugar
350ml/12fl oz/1½ cups water
1 lemon
450g/1lb each eating apples, pears, and peaches or nectarines
350g/12oz seedless green grapes
4 oranges

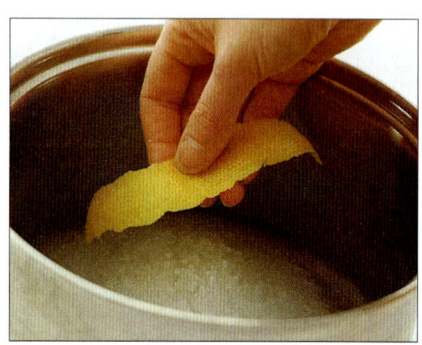

1 Put the sugar and water in a pan. Pare off a small strip of lemon rind, avoiding the pith, and add to the pan. Heat gently, stirring, until the sugar has dissolved. Bring to the boil and simmer for 1 minute. Cover and leave to stand.

2 Halve the lemon, then squeeze out the juice and strain.

3 Prepare the fruit, allowing 275g/10oz fruit for each 450g/1lb jar. Peel, core and slice the apples and pears and toss in lemon juice. Peel, halve, stone (pit) and slice the peaches or nectarines; halve the grapes; and segment the oranges.

4 Rinse hot sterilized jars with boiling water. Pack the fruit into the jars tightly, pressing down gently with a wooden spoon.

5 Strain the syrup through a fine sieve and return it to the cleaned pan. Bring to the boil, then pour over the fruit, filling the jars to within 1cm/½in of the top. Cover and heat-treat.

making poached pears

Fruit is often poached in syrup until just tender before bottling.

Makes about 1.8kg/4lb

INGREDIENTS
225g/8oz/scant 1¼ cups granulated sugar
1.2 litres/2 pints/5 cups water
1 orange
1 cinnamon stick
2kg/4½ lb cooking pears

1 Put the sugar and water in a large, wide pan and add a thinly pared strip of orange rind and the cinnamon. Heat gently until the sugar has dissolved, then bring to the boil and simmer for 1 minute.

2 Squeeze the juice from the orange, then strain. Peel and core the pears, then toss in lemon juice as soon as each one is prepared.

3 Add the pears to the syrup in a single layer. Place greaseproof (waxed) paper over the pears to keep them immersed. Poach for 15 minutes until just tender and slightly translucent; the syrup should hardly bubble so that the fruit holds its shape. Once cooked, bottle and heat-treat.

MAKING SUGAR SYRUPS
Poach whole and slightly hard fruits such as pears and plums in a light syrup; poach figs, peaches, nectarines and apricots in a medium syrup; and poach soft fruits such as strawberries and raspberries in a heavy syrup.

To make a light syrup, use 115g/4oz/generous ½ cup sugar to 600ml/1 pint/2½ cups water; to make a medium syrup, use 175g/6oz/scant 1 cup sugar to 600ml/1 pint/2½ cups water; to make a heavy syrup, use 350g/12oz/1¾ cups sugar to 600ml/1 pint/2½ cups water.

Put the sugar and water in a pan and heat gently, stirring, until the sugar has dissolved. Bring to the boil and simmer for 1 minute. Use hot or cool.

HEAT TREATMENT

There are several ways to heat-treat bottled fruit. The filled jars may be heated in hot water, in the oven, or in a pressure cooker. As the fruit cools, a vacuum is created.

Use jars specifically designed for heat treatment. Preserving jars with clamp tops should be sealed once filled; the clamps expand slightly to allow steam to escape. Screw tops on preserving jars should not be tightened until after heating because the steam will not be able to escape and the jars may burst. Heat-treated preserves may be kept for up to 2 years.

water bath method

This is suitable for fruits bottled in either hot or cold syrup; the latter will take a little longer to process.

1 Wrap folded newspaper or cloth around each filled container, then stand them on a metal trivet or a thick layer of paper or cloth in a large heavy pan. (Containers placed directly on the pan may crack.)

2 Pour tepid water around the jars, right up to the neck, then cover the pan. Bring slowly to the boil (this should take 25–30 minutes), then simmer for the required time.

3 Turn off the heat and ladle out some of the hot water. Using tongs or oven gloves, lift the containers out of the pan and place on a wooden board. If they have screw-band lids, tighten immediately.

4 Leave the containers to cool for 24 hours, then remove the screw bands or clips. Holding the rim of the lid, carefully lift the container; it should hold its own weight. Containers with one-piece lids should have a very slight dip in the lid to indicate that they are sealed. If a jar is not sealed properly, it should be stored in the refrigerator and used as soon as possible.

HEATING TIMES FOR THE WATER BATH METHOD

The following times are for fruit packed in hot syrup after boiling. Allow 5 minutes more for fruit packed in cold syrup.

Fruit	Minutes
Soft berries and redcurrants	2
Blackcurrants, gooseberries, rhubarb, cherries, apricots and plums	10
Peaches and nectarines	20
Figs and pears	35

moderate oven method

This is only suitable for fruits covered with hot syrup; cold-filled jars may crack in the warm oven.

1 Preheat the oven to 150°C/300°F/Gas 2. Put the rubber rings and lids on the filled jars, but do not seal. Place in a roasting pan lined with newspaper or cloth, spacing the jars about 5cm/2in apart. Pour 1cm/½in boiling water into the pan.

2 Place the pan in the middle of the oven. Cook 500–600ml/17–20fl oz jars for 30–35 minutes and 1 litre/1¾ pint jars for 35–55 minutes. If there are more than four jars, allow a little extra time.

3 Remove from the oven and seal the lids immediately. Cool on a wooden board. Test the seals as for the water bath method.

pressure cooker method

If using clip-top jars, move the clips slightly to the side of the lid to reduce the pressure. Check the instructions for the pressure cooker.

1 Stand the jars on the trivet in the pressure cooker, ensuring they do not touch each other or the pan.

2 Pour in 600ml/1 pint/2½ cups hot water. Put on the lid with a low (2.25kg/5lb) weight and slowly bring to pressure. Maintain this pressure for 4 minutes. Leave to stand until the pressure drops.

3 Transfer the jars to a board and seal. Leave for 12 hours, then test as for the water bath method.

MAKING CANDIED AND GLACÉ FRUIT

Sugar is an excellent preservative. Candying is a method by which fruit or citrus peel is preserved by steeping in syrup. The fruit or peel becomes so saturated in sugar that natural deterioration is virtually halted. The process works by gradually replacing the fruit's moisture with a saturated sugar solution. This has to be done slowly and takes at least 15 days, but is well worth it. Candied fruit is expensive to buy and, although you need to plan ahead when making candied fruit or peel, it requires only a little time each day.

making candied fruit

You can candy as much or as little fruit as you like, working with the basic proportions of fruit to sugar given in the recipe below. Always candy different fruits separately, so that each type retains its own flavour. Choose firm, fresh fruits that are free of blemishes.

INGREDIENTS
fresh, firm, just-ripe fruit, such as pineapples, peaches, pears, apples, plums, apricots, kiwi fruit or cherries
granulated sugar
caster (superfine) sugar, for sprinkling

Day 1

1 Prepare the fruit. Thickly peel and core pineapples, then slice into rings; peel, stone (pit) or core peaches, pears and apples, then halve or cut into thick slices; plums and apricots can be left whole (prick them all over with a fine skewer) or halve and stone; skin and quarter kiwi fruits, or thickly slice; stone cherries.

2 Weigh the fruit, then put in a pan and just cover with water. Bring to the boil and simmer until just tender. Do not overcook because the flavour and shape will be lost; do not undercook because the fruit will be tough when candied.

3 Using a slotted spoon, lift the cooked fruit into a large wide bowl; avoid piling the fruit up high. Retain the cooking liquid.

4 For every 450g/1lb prepared (uncooked) fruit, use 300ml/½ pint/ 1¼ cups of the cooking liquid and 175g/6oz/scant 1 cup sugar. Gently heat the sugar and liquid in a pan, stirring, until the sugar has dissolved, then bring to the boil.

5 Pour the boiling syrup over the fruit, making sure that the fruit is completely immersed. Cover and leave to stand for 24 hours.

Day 2

1 Drain the syrup from the fruit back into a pan, being careful not to damage the fruit as you do so. Return the fruit to the bowl.

2 Add 50g/2oz/¼ cup granulated sugar to the syrup and heat gently, stirring until dissolved completely, then bring to the boil.

3 Pour the hot syrup over the fruit. Allow to cool, then cover and leave to stand for 24 hours.

Days 3–7

Repeat the instructions for day 2 every day for the next 5 days. The concentration of sugar will become much stronger.

Days 8–9

1 Drain the syrup from the fruit into a large wide pan and add 90g/3½oz/½ cup sugar. Heat gently, stirring, until dissolved.

2 Carefully add the fruit to the syrup and simmer gently for about 3 minutes. Return the fruit and syrup to the bowl, cool, then cover and leave to stand for 48 hours.

Days 10–13

Repeat the instructions for days 8–9, leaving the fruit to soak for 4 days rather than 2.

COOK'S TIP

The final soaking stage from days 10–13 can be extended another 6 days, if you like – to a total of 10 days. The longer the fruit is left to soak in the syrup, the sweeter and more intense its flavour will become.

Days 14–15

1 Drain the fruit, discarding the syrup. Carefully spread the fruit out, spacing each piece slightly apart, on a wire rack placed over a baking sheet.

2 Cut a sheet of baking parchment or foil slightly larger than the baking sheet. Using a fine skewer, prick about 12 tiny holes at equal intervals in the sheet.

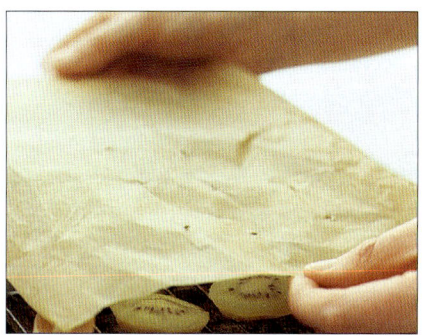

3 Cover the fruit with the baking parchment or foil, being very careful not to touch the fruit. The parchment or foil is simply to keep off any dust; some air should still be able to circulate around the fruit.

4 Leave the fruit in a warm place such as a sunny windowsill or airing cupboard for 2 days, turning each piece of fruit occasionally until all the fruit is thoroughly dry.

5 Sprinkle the fruit with a little caster sugar, then store in an airtight container in single layers between sheets of greaseproof (waxed) paper. Eat within 1 year.

COOK'S TIP

Candied fruits are very pretty, retaining the colour of the original fruits. They make great sweetmeats for serving after a meal, particularly at Christmas.

making candied peel

Citrus peel contains less moisture than the fruit, making candying simpler and less time-consuming.

INGREDIENTS

5 small oranges, 6 lemons or 7 limes, or a combination

granulated sugar

caster (superfine) sugar, for sprinkling

1 Scrub the fruit. Remove the peel in quarters, scraping away the pith. Place in a pan, cover with cold water and simmer for 1¼–1½ hours. Drain, reserving 300ml/½ pint/1¼ cups of the cooking water.

2 Pour the reserved water into the pan and add 200g/7oz/1 cup sugar. Heat gently, stirring until dissolved, then bring to the boil. Add the peel and simmer for 1 minute. Leave to cool, tip into a bowl, cover and leave for 48 hours.

3 Remove the peel and pour the syrup back into the pan. Add 150g/5oz/¾ cup sugar and heat gently, stirring until dissolved. Add the peel, bring to the boil, then simmer until transparent. Cool, pour into a bowl, cover and leave for 2 weeks.

4 Drain the peel, then dry, sprinkle and store in the same way as candied fruit.

making glacé fruit

Glacé, or crystallized, fruit is made from candied fruit, dipped in heavy syrup to give it a glossy coating.

INGREDIENTS

candied fruit

400g/14oz/2 cups granulated sugar

120ml/4fl oz/½ cup water

1 Make sure the candied fruit is dry and dust off any sugar coating. Put the sugar and water in a pan and heat gently, stirring, until the sugar has completely dissolved. Bring to the boil and simmer for 2 minutes.

2 Pour one-third of the syrup into a small bowl. Fill a second bowl with boiling water. Using a slotted spoon or fork, first dip the fruit into the boiling water for 15 seconds, then shake and dip into the syrup for 15 seconds. Place on a wire rack.

3 Repeat with the remaining fruit, topping up the bowl of syrup when necessary (return the syrup to the boil before doing this); replace the bowl of boiling water once or twice.

4 Dry the fruit on wire racks placed over baking sheets in a very warm place for 2–3 days, turning the fruit occasionally. Store in the same way as candied fruit.

MAKING DRIED FRUITS AND VEGETABLES

Removing moisture from foods is one of the oldest methods of preserving. Traditional techniques depend on the correct proportions of sunlight, heat and humidity for successful results. If food is dried too fast, moisture can get trapped and spoil it; if it is dried too slowly, micro-organisms may start to grow. Most commercially dried fruits and vegetables, such as apricots, figs and tomatoes, which are high both in sugar and acid, are still wind- and sun-dried in the way they have been for centuries.

To re-create these conditions, an airy place with a steady temperature is needed. A very warm room or cupboard may be used if the temperature is constant, but the most efficient way is to use an oven on the lowest setting.

A fan oven is ideal because of the constant circulation of air. If using a conventional oven, leave the door open with the tiniest possible gap, or open frequently during the drying process to let steam escape. Be careful that the temperature does not become too high, or the fruit or vegetables will cook and shrivel. If necessary, turn off the oven occasionally and leave it to cool down.

Choose firm, fresh and ripe fruit and vegetables for drying. Citrus fruits and melons consist mainly of water, so do not dry well, nor do berry fruits because they discolour and become very seedy. To help preserve the dried fruit and prevent discoloration, the prepared pieces should be dipped into a very weak brine solution, or acidulated water, before drying.

making dried apple rings

INGREDIENTS
15ml/1 tbsp salt, or 90ml/6 tbsp lemon juice, or 30ml/2 tbsp ascorbic acid (vitamin C) powder
1.2 litres/2 pints/5 cups water
900g/2lb firm, ripe apples

1 Put the salt, lemon juice or ascorbic acid powder in a large bowl and pour in the water. Stir until dissolved.

2 Peel and core the apples, then cut into rings slightly thicker than 5mm/¼in. As soon as each apple is cut, put the rings in the bowl of water and leave for 1 minute before lifting out. Pat the rings dry using kitchen paper.

3 Thread the apple rings on to wooden skewers, leaving a small space between each ring, or spread the apple rings out on wire racks. (Baking sheets are not suitable because air needs to circulate around the fruit.)

4 If using skewers, rest them on the oven shelves, allowing the apple rings to hang between the gaps. If using wire racks, simply place the racks in the oven. Leave the door very slightly ajar.

5 Dry the apples at 110°C/225°F/Gas ¼ for about 5 hours, or until the apple rings resemble soft, pliable leather.

6 Remove the fruit from the oven and leave to cool completely. Very crisp fruits and vegetables should be stored in airtight containers, but leathery, pliable fruits are better stored in paper bags or cardboard boxes; storing them in plastic bags may make them go mouldy.

7 To reconstitute the dried apple slices, put them in a bowl and pour over boiling water. Leave to soak for at least 5 minutes, then place in a pan and gently cook in the soaking liquid.

COOK'S TIPS
• Dried apple slices make a healthy snack and are popular with children.
• They are also good chopped and added to desserts and cakes.

PRESERVING FRUITS IN ALCOHOL

Fruits preserved in alcohol make luxurious instant desserts, served with crème fraîche or ice cream. One of the best-known fruit and alcohol preserves is German *rumtopf*, which means rum pot. It consists of summer and early autumn fruits bottled in alcohol, usually rum, but not always, with a little sugar. Traditionally, this preserve is made in a large jar with a wide neck and tight-fitting lid.

Pure alcohol is the best preservative because bacteria and moulds are unable to grow in it. Clear liqueurs, such as eau de vie, orange liqueur, Kirsch and Amaretto, or spirits such as brandy, rum and vodka, which are at least 40% ABV, may be used.

The alcohol content of table wine and cider is too low and so these are not effective preservatives on their own unless the bottles are heat-treated. Fruits preserved in wine or cider should be stored in the refrigerator and used within 1 month of making.

When using alcohol to preserve, it is usually best to combine it with sugar syrup because high-alcohol liqueurs and spirits tend to shrink the fruit. Most fruits are first simmered in syrup, which helps to tenderize the fruit and kills the bad enzymes.

The type of syrup used for preserving fruits in alcohol varies depending on the sweetness and juiciness of the fruit, as well as the desired result. A typical syrup would be 600ml/1 pint/2½ cups alcohol, blended with a syrup of 150ml/¼ pint/⅔ cup water and 150g/5oz/¾ cup sugar.

making nectarines in brandy syrup

For extra flavour, you can add whole spices such as vanilla or cinnamon to the syrup.

Makes about 900g/2lb

INGREDIENTS

350g/12oz/1¾ cups preserving or granulated sugar
150ml/¼ pint/⅔ cup water
450g/1lb firm, ripe nectarines
2 bay leaves
150ml/¼ pint/⅔ cup brandy

1 Put the sugar in a large heavy pan with the water and heat gently, stirring until dissolved completely. Bring to the boil, then reduce the heat and simmer for 10 minutes.

2 Halve and stone (pit) the nectarines. (If liked, you may also peel them.) Add them to the syrup.

3 Reduce the heat so that the syrup is barely simmering and poach the nectarines until almost tender. Add the bay leaves 1 minute before the end of the cooking. Turn off the heat and leave them to stand for 5 minutes; they will cook a little more as it cools.

4 Using a slotted spoon, lift the fruit out of the pan and pack into hot sterilized jars.

5 Bring the syrup to a rapid boil and cook for 3–4 minutes. Leave to cool for a few minutes, then stir in the brandy. (Do not add the brandy to the boiling syrup because the alcohol will evaporate and the syrup will lose its preserving qualities.) Pour the syrup into the jars, covering the fruit completely. Tap the jars to release any air and seal. Store in a cool dark place and use within 1 year.

MODERN PRESERVING TECHNIQUES

With the advent of new kitchen equipment such as microwaves, pressure cookers and freezers, new ways to make fruit preserves have developed. The increased concern over healthy eating has also led to new types of preserves such as reduced-sugar jams.

PRESERVING IN A MICROWAVE

Preserves can be made using a microwave, but only using specific recipes intended for the appliance. It is difficult to adapt conventional recipes because many rely on the evaporation of liquid to achieve a set or to thicken the preserve.

Make sure the ingredients are at room temperature; if they are not, it will affect cooking times. Frozen fruit can be used to make microwave preserves, but it must be defrosted first.

Chop fruit into equal-size pieces so that they cook at the same speed, and stir the preserve frequently during cooking to distribute the heat evenly and avoid hot spots. Use a suitable microwave-proof bowl that will withstand very hot temperatures, and that is large enough to hold twice the volume of the ingredients.

When the preserve has finished cooking, leave it to stand for several minutes until it has stopped bubbling. It is essential to protect your hands with oven gloves when lifting the bowl; take care not to place it on a cold surface because this may cause the glass to crack – a wooden board is ideal for protecting the surface and bowl.

making microwave lemon curd

This recipe is based on an 800 watt microwave. For microwaves with a different wattage, adjust cooking times as follows – for a 900 watt oven: subtract 10 seconds per minute; for a 850 watt oven: subtract 5 seconds per minute; for a 750 watt oven: add 5 seconds per minute; for a 700 watt oven: add 10 seconds per minute.

Makes about 450g/1lb

INGREDIENTS

115g/4oz/½ cup butter, cubed
finely grated rind and juice of 3 large lemons
225g/8oz/generous 1 cup caster (superfine) sugar
3 eggs plus 1 egg yolk

1 Put the butter, lemon rind and juice in a large microwave-proof bowl. Cook on high for 3 minutes.

2 Add the sugar to the bowl and stir for 1 minute until it has almost dissolved. Return to the microwave and cook on 100% power for 2 minutes, stirring every 1 minute.

3 Beat the eggs and the yolk together, then whisk into the lemon mixture, a little at a time.

4 Cook on 40% power, for 10–12 minutes, whisking every 2 minutes, until the curd thickens. Ladle into hot sterilized jars, cover and seal. When cool, store in the refrigerator. Use within 2 months.

PRESERVING USING A PRESSURE COOKER

Preserves can be made very quickly using a pressure cooker. They are particularly useful for marmalades and for softening whole or hard fruits. Never fill the pan more than half full and always check the manufacturer's instructions.

making pressure-cooker orange marmalade

Makes about 2.5kg/5½lb

INGREDIENTS

900g/2lb Seville (Temple) oranges
1 large lemon
1.2 litres/2 pints/5 cups water
1.8kg/4lb/generous 9 cups preserving or granulated sugar

1 Scrub the fruit, then halve and squeeze out the juice, retaining any pips. Quarter the oranges, scrape off the pulp and membranes and tie in a piece of muslin (cheesecloth) with the lemon halves and any pips.

2 Place the orange peel in the pressure cooker with the muslin bag and 900ml/1½ pints/3¾ cups of the water. Bring to medium (4.5kg/10lb) pressure and cook for 10 minutes.

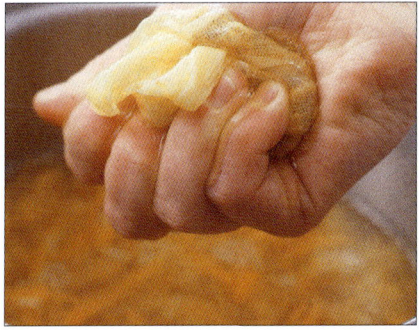

3 Reduce the pressure and leave until the fruit is cool enough to handle. Remove the muslin bag and squeeze it over the pan.

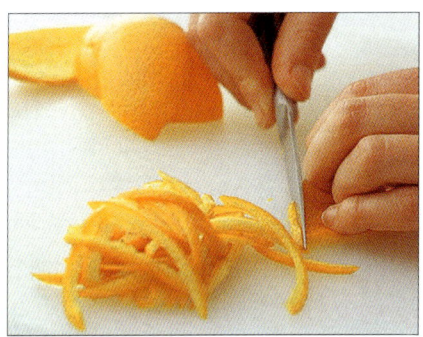

4 Cut the orange peel into fine shreds and return to the pan with the remaining water and the fruit juice. Add the sugar and heat gently until the sugar has dissolved. Bring to the boil, then boil rapidly for about 10 minutes until setting point is reached (105°C/220°F).

5 Remove any scum from the surface using a slotted spoon, then leave the marmalade to cool until a thin skin starts to form on the surface. Stir gently to distribute the peel evenly, then ladle into hot sterilized jars, cover and seal.

MAKING FREEZER JAMS

This type of jam is not cooked, so it has a fresher, fruitier flavour and a brighter colour than cooked jam. Once thawed, it does not keep as well as traditional jam. Commercial pectin is used as a setting agent.

making strawberry freezer jam

Makes about 1.3kg/3lb

INGREDIENTS

800g/1¾lb/7 cups strawberries
900g/2lb/4½ cups caster (superfine) sugar
30ml/2 tbsp lemon juice
120ml/4fl oz/½ cup commercial liquid pectin

1 Wipe the fruit. (Only wash if necessary, then pat dry on kitchen paper.) Hull and cut into quarters, then put in a bowl with the sugar.

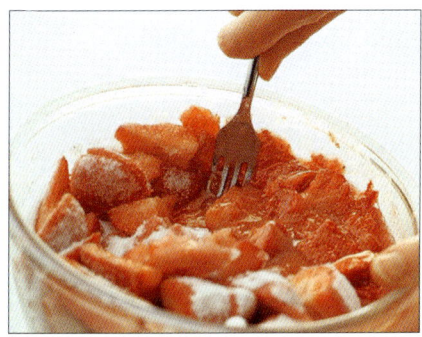

2 Lightly mash the fruit with a fork, leaving plenty of lumps of fruit. Cover and leave to stand for 1 hour, stirring once or twice.

3 Add the lemon juice and pectin to the fruit and stir for 4 minutes until thoroughly combined. Ladle the jam into small freezer-proof containers, cover and leave to stand for about 4 hours.

4 Put the jam in the refrigerator and chill for 24–48 hours, or until the jam sets. Freeze the jam for up to 6 months, or until ready to use.

5 To serve, remove the jam from the freezer and leave at room temperature for about 1 hour, or until defrosted. Keep any leftover defrosted jam in the refrigerator and use quickly.

MAKING REDUCED-SUGAR PRESERVES

Sugar is the vital preserving agent in sweet fruit preserves. It helps to prevent fermentation and spoilage, as well as adding sweetness and flavour, and improving the set. The proportion of sugar required for this is about 60 per cent of the final weight of preserve. Although it is possible to make reduced-sugar preserves, the yield is smaller and they will not keep for as long. In most recipes, the sugar content can be reduced by up to half. The jam should be stored in the refrigerator and used within 4 months.

USING FROZEN FRUIT

Freezing is a quick and convenient way to preserve fruit when it is at its best and cheapest. It is especially useful for fruit with a very short season, such as Seville or Temple oranges. Freezing does destroy some of the pectin content, so to compensate for this, an extra 10 per cent of fruit should be used in the recipe. Do a pectin test during cooking to check the set.

jams and conserves

Preserving fruits in jams and conserves is one of the best ways of enjoying their delicious flavour all year round. In summer, with its long, warm days, there is an abundance of sweet juicy berries, while the autumn harvest offers a fabulous choice of stone and hedgerow fruits. All of these can be made into irresistible jams that can be enjoyed at any time of day – spread on toast, used as a filling or topping for plain cakes, or spooned over ice cream for a treat. All the recipes in this chapter will keep for at least 6 months.

seedless raspberry and passion fruit jam

The pips in raspberry jam can often put people off this wonderful preserve. This version has none of the pips and all of the flavour, and is enhanced by the tangy addition of passion fruit.

Makes about 1.3kg/3lb

INGREDIENTS

1.6kg/3½lb/14 cups raspberries

4 passion fruit, halved

1.3kg/3lb/6½ cups preserving sugar with pectin, warmed

juice of 1 lemon

COOK'S TIPS

• Check the instructions on the sugar packet for details of the boiling time.

• If you cannot find preserving sugar with pectin, use the same quantity of regular sugar and add powdered or liquid pectin. Check the instructions on the packet for quantities.

1 Place the raspberries in a large pan, then scoop out the passion fruit seeds and pulp and add to the raspberries. Cover and cook over a low heat for 20 minutes, or until the juices begin to run.

2 Remove the pan from the heat and leave to cool slightly, then, using the back of a spoon, press the fruit through a coarse sieve (strainer) into a preserving pan.

3 Add the sugar and lemon juice to the pan and stir over a low heat until the sugar has dissolved. Bring to the boil and cook for 4 minutes, or until the jam reaches setting point (105°C/220°F).

4 Remove the pan from the heat and skim off any scum. Leave to cool slightly, then pour into warmed sterilized jars. Seal and label, then store in a cool place.

34 • jams and conserves

wild strawberry and rose petal conserve

This fragrant jam is ideal served with summer cream teas. Rose water complements the strawberries beautifully, but only add a few drops because the flavour can easily become overpowering.

Makes about 900g/2lb

INGREDIENTS

900g/2lb/8 cups wild Alpine strawberries

450g/1lb/4 cups strawberries, hulled and mashed

2 dark pink rose buds, petals only

juice of 2 lemons

1.3kg/3lb/6½ cups granulated sugar, warmed

a few drops of rose water

1 Put all the strawberries in a non-metallic bowl with the rose petals, lemon juice and warmed sugar. Cover and leave overnight.

2 The next day, tip the fruit into a preserving pan and heat gently, stirring, until all the sugar has dissolved. Boil for 10–15 minutes, or to setting point (105°C/220°F).

3 Stir the rose water into the jam, then remove the pan from the heat. Skim off any scum and leave to cool for 5 minutes, then stir and pour into warmed sterilized jars. Seal and label, then store.

COOK'S TIPS

• If you are unable to find wild berries, use ordinary strawberries instead. Leave the smaller berries whole but mash any large ones.

• To make plain strawberry jam, make in the same way but leave out the rose petals and rose water.

jams and conserves • 35

blueberry and lime jam

The subtle yet fragrant flavour of blueberries can be elusive on its own. Adding a generous quantity of tangy lime juice enhances their flavour and gives this jam a wonderful zesty taste.

Makes about 1.3kg/3lb

INGREDIENTS

1.3kg/3lb/12 cups blueberries

finely pared rind and juice of 4 limes

1kg/2¼lb/5 cups preserving sugar with pectin

COOK'S TIP

Blueberries are not naturally high in pectin, so extra pectin is needed for a good set. If you prefer, used granulated sugar and add pectin according to the instruction on the packet in place of the preserving sugar with pectin.

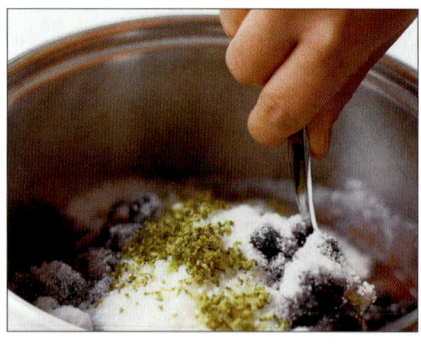

1 Put the blueberries, lime juice and half the sugar in a large, non-metallic bowl and lightly crush the berries using a potato masher. Set aside for about 4 hours.

2 Tip the crushed berry mixture into a pan and stir in the finely pared lime rind and the remaining preserving sugar. Heat slowly, stirring continuously, until the sugar has completely dissolved.

3 Increase the heat and bring to the boil. Boil rapidly for about 4 minutes, or until the jam reaches setting point (105°C/220°F).

4 Remove the pan from the heat and set aside for 5 minutes. Stir the jam gently, then pour into warmed sterilized jars. Seal the jars, then label when completely cool. Store in a cool, dark place.

blackcurrant jam

This jam has a rich, fruity flavour and a wonderfully strong dark colour. It is punchy and delicious with scones for tea or spread on croissants for a continental-style breakfast.

Makes about 1.3kg/3lb

INGREDIENTS

1.3kg/3lb/12 cups blackcurrants
grated rind and juice of 1 orange
475ml/16fl oz/2 cups water
1.3kg/3lb/6½ cups granulated sugar, warmed
30ml/2 tbsp cassis (optional)

1 Place the blackcurrants, orange rind and juice and water in a large heavy pan. Bring to the boil, reduce the heat and simmer for 30 minutes.

2 Add the warmed sugar to the pan and stir over a low heat until the sugar has dissolved.

3 Bring the mixture to the boil and cook for about 8 minutes, or until the jam reaches setting point (105°C/220°F).

4 Remove the pan from the heat and skim off any scum from the surface using a slotted spoon. Leave to cool for 5 minutes, then stir in the cassis, if using.

5 Pour the jam into warmed sterilized jars and seal. Leave the jars to cool completely, then label and store in a cool, dark place.

jams and conserves • 37

dried apricot jam

This richly flavoured jam can be made at any time of year, so even if you miss the short apricot season, you can still enjoy the delicious taste of sweet, tangy apricot jam all year round.

Makes about 2kg/4½lb

INGREDIENTS

675g/1½lb dried apricots

900ml/1½ pints/3¾ cups apple juice

juice and grated rind of 2 unwaxed lemons

675g/1½lb/scant 3½ cups preserving or granulated sugar, warmed

50g/2oz/½ cup blanched almonds, coarsely chopped

COOK'S TIP

Use the best quality traditional dried apricots to make this jam. They have a more suitable texture than the soft ready-to-eat dried apricots and will produce a better end result.

1 Put the apricots in a bowl, pour over the apple juice and leave to soak overnight.

2 Pour the soaked apricots and juice into a preserving pan and add the lemon juice and rind. Bring to the boil, then lower the heat and simmer for 15–20 minutes until the apricots are soft.

3 Add the warmed sugar to the pan and bring to the boil, stirring until the sugar has completely dissolved. Boil for 15–20 minutes, or until setting point is reached (105°C/220°F).

4 Stir the chopped almonds into the jam and leave to stand for about 15 minutes, then pour the jam into warmed, sterilized jars. Seal, then leave to cool completely before labelling. Store in a cool, dark place.

peach and amaretto jam

Adding amaretto (almond liqueur) produces a luxurious jam that's perfect served on warm buttered toast or English muffins. You can use peach schnapps in place of the amaretto if you prefer.

Makes about 1.3kg/3lb

INGREDIENTS
1.3kg/3lb peaches
250ml/8fl oz/1 cup water
juice of 2 lemons
1.3kg/3lb/6½ cups granulated sugar, warmed
45ml/3 tbsp amaretto liqueur

1 Carefully peel the peaches using a vegetable peeler, or blanch briefly in boiling water, then peel with a knife. Reserve the skins.

2 Halve and stone (pit) the fruit, dice the flesh and put in a pan with the water. Place the skins in a small pan with water to cover. Boil until the liquid is reduced to 30ml/2 tbsp. Press the skins and liquid through a sieve into the peaches. Cover and simmer for 20 minutes, or until soft.

3 Add the lemon juice and sugar to the pan. Heat, stirring, until the sugar has dissolved completely. Bring to the boil and cook for 10–15 minutes, or to setting point (105°C/220°F). Remove from the heat and skim off any scum from the surface using a slotted spoon.

4 Leave the jam to cool for about 10 minutes, then stir in the amaretto and pour into warmed sterilized jars. Seal, then leave to cool completely before labelling. Store in a cool, dark place.

jams and conserves

gooseberry and elderflower jam

Pale green gooseberries and fragrant elderflowers make perfect partners in this sharp, aromatic, intensely flavoured jam. The jam turns an unexpected pink colour during cooking.

Makes about 2kg/4½lb

INGREDIENTS

1.3kg/3lb/12 cups firm gooseberries, topped and tailed

300ml/½ pint/1¼ cups water

1.3kg/3lb/6½ cups granulated sugar, warmed

juice of 1 lemon

2 handfuls of elderflowers removed from their stalks

1 Put the gooseberries into a large preserving pan, add the water and bring the mixture to the boil.

2 Cover the pan with a lid and simmer gently for 20 minutes until the fruit is soft. Using a potato masher, gently mash the fruit to crush it lightly.

3 Add the sugar, lemon juice and elderflowers to the pan and stir over a low heat until the sugar has dissolved. Boil for 10 minutes, or to setting point (105°C/220°F). Remove from the heat, skim off any scum and cool for 5 minutes, then stir. Pot and seal, then leave to cool before labelling.

COOK'S TIP

The time taken to reach setting point will vary depending on the ripeness of the gooseberries. The riper the fruit, the longer the jam will need to be cooked to reach setting point.

damson jam

Dark, plump damsons used to only be found growing in the wild, but today they are available commercially. They produce a deeply coloured and richly flavoured jam that makes a delicious treat spread on toasted English muffins or warm crumpets at tea time.

Makes about 2kg/4½lb

INGREDIENTS

1kg/2¼lb damsons or wild plums

1.4 litres/2½ pints/6 cups water

1kg/2¼lb/5 cups preserving or granulated sugar, warmed

COOK'S TIP

It is important to seal the jars as soon as you have filled them to ensure the jam remains sterile. However, you should then leave the jars to cool completely before labelling and storing them to avoid the risk of burns.

1 Put the damsons in a preserving pan and pour in the water. Bring to the boil. Reduce the heat and simmer gently until the damsons are soft, then stir in the sugar.

2 Bring the mixture to the boil, skimming off stones as they rise. Boil to setting point (105°C/220°F). Leave to cool for 10 minutes, then pot. Seal, then label and store when cool.

greengage and almond jam

This is the perfect preserve to make when greengages are readily available in stores, or if you find you have a glut of the fruit. It has a gloriously rich, golden honey colour and a smooth texture that contrasts wonderfully with the little slivers of almond.

Makes about 1.3kg/3lb

INGREDIENTS

1.3kg/3lb greengages, stoned (pitted)
350ml/12fl oz/1½ cups water
juice of 1 lemon
50g/2oz/½ cup blanched almonds, cut into thin slivers
1.3kg/3lb/6½ cups granulated sugar, warmed

COOK'S TIP

Greengages look like unripened plums. However, despite their appearance, they have a wonderfully aromatic flavour that is captured perfectly in this delicious jam.

1 Put the greengages and water in a preserving pan with the lemon juice and almond slivers. Bring to the boil, then cover and simmer for 15–20 minutes, or until the greengages are really soft.

2 Add the sugar to the pan and stir over a low heat until the sugar has dissolved. Bring to the boil and cook for 10–15 minutes, or until the jam reaches setting point (105°C/220°F).

3 Remove the pan from the heat and skim off any scum from the surface using a slotted spoon.

4 Leave to cool for 10 minutes, then stir gently and pour into warmed sterilized jars. Seal, then leave to cool completely before labelling. Store in a cool place.

rhubarb and ginger jam

Late summer is the time to make this preserve, when rhubarb leaves are enormous and the stalks thick and green. It has a wonderfully tart, tangy flavour and is delicious spooned over plain cake, or used as a filling with whipped cream.

Makes about 2kg/4½lb

INGREDIENTS

1kg/2¼lb rhubarb

1kg/2¼lb/5 cups preserving or granulated sugar

25g/1oz fresh root ginger, bruised

115g/4oz crystallized ginger

50g/2oz/¼ cup candied orange peel, chopped

COOK'S TIP

The young, slender rhubarb stems that are available in the spring are more suitable for making tarts and pies. Their delicate flavour does not shine through in preserves, so it is worth waiting until later in the season for mature rhubarb.

1 Cut the rhubarb into short pieces and layer with the sugar in a glass bowl. Leave to stand overnight.

2 The next day, scrape the rhubarb and sugar mixture into a large, heavy preserving pan.

3 Tie the bruised ginger root in a piece of muslin (cheesecloth) and add it to the rhubarb. Cook gently for 30 minutes, or until the rhubarb has softened.

4 Remove the root ginger from the pan and stir in the crystallized ginger and candied orange peel.

5 Bring the mixture to the boil, then cook over a high heat until setting point is reached (105°C/220°F). Leave to cool for a few minutes, then pour into warmed sterilized jars and seal. When completely cool, label and store.

jams and conserves • 43

sweet fruit jellies

Sparkling, jewel-like sweet fruit jellies make a wonderful alternative to jams and conserves, spread on toast or crumpets, or spooned over ice cream in place of a sauce. The fruit is cooked gently for as short a time as possible, then strained through muslin to obtain the clear liquid. Jellies give a lower yield than jam but they really capture the true flavour of fruits and are a lovely way to preserve.

hedgerow jelly

In the autumn, hedgerows are laden with damsons, blackberries and elderberries and it is well worth spending an afternoon in the countryside picking fruit to make into this delightful jelly.

Makes about 1.3kg/3lb

INGREDIENTS

450g/1lb damsons, washed
450g/1lb/4 cups blackberries, washed
225g/8oz/2 cups raspberries
225g/8oz/2 cups elderberries, washed
juice and pips (seeds) of 2 large lemons
about 1.3kg/3lb/6½ cups preserving or granulated sugar, warmed

COOK'S TIP

If you do not have enough of one fruit, you can vary the quantities as long as the total weight of fruit is the same.

1 Put the fruit, lemon juice and pips into a large pan. Add water to just below the level of the fruit. Cover and simmer for 1 hour.

2 Mash the fruit and leave to cool slightly. Pour into a scalded jelly bag suspended over a non-metallic bowl and leave to drain overnight.

3 Measure the strained juice into a preserving pan. Add 450g/1lb/ 2¼ cups sugar for every 600ml/ 1 pint/2½ cups strained fruit juice.

4 Heat the mixture, stirring, over a low heat until the sugar has dissolved. Increase the heat and boil rapidly without stirring for 10–15 minutes, or until the jelly reaches setting point (105°C/220°F).

5 Remove the pan from the heat and skim off any scum using a slotted spoon. Ladle into warmed, sterilized jars and seal. Leave to cool, then label and store.

mulberry jelly

Deep red mulberries are not often available but if you have access to a tree you will find they make the most wonderful jellies and jams. For a good set, pick the fruits when they are red.

Makes about 900g/2lb

INGREDIENTS

900g/2lb/8 cups unripe red mulberries
grated rind and juice of 1 lemon
600ml/1 pint/2½ cups water
about 900g/2lb/4½ cups preserving
  or granulated sugar, warmed

1 Put the mulberries in a pan with the lemon rind and juice and the water. Bring to the boil, cover and simmer for 1 hour, then remove from the heat and leave to cool.

2 Pour the fruit into a scalded jelly bag suspended over a non-metallic bowl and leave to drain overnight.

3 Measure the strained juice into a preserving pan. Add 450g/1lb/ 2¼ cups sugar for every 600ml/ 1 pint/2½ cups fruit juice.

4 Heat the mixture over a low heat, stirring, until the sugar has completely dissolved. Increase the heat and boil rapidly, without stirring, for 5–10 minutes, or to setting point (105°C/220°F).

5 Skim off any scum from the surface of the jelly using a slotted spoon. Ladle into warmed, sterilized jars, cover and seal. When the jars are completely cool, label, then store in a cool, dark place.

COOK'S TIPS

• To test for the set, spoon a little jelly on to a chilled saucer. Chill for about 3 minutes, then gently push the jelly with your finger; if the surface wrinkles, the jelly has reached setting point and it is ready to bottle.

• To make redcurrant jelly using the method here, measure the same quantity of fruit, but add slightly less sugar to the strained juice: 450g/ 1lb/1¼ cups sugar for every 600ml/ 1 pint/2½ cups juice.

sweet fruit jellies • 47

cranberry jelly

This clear, well-flavoured preserve has a tart flavour and is absolutely delicious served with freshly baked scones, toasted tea cakes and crumpets, or as a glaze for fruit tarts. It can also be served at Christmas with a festive roast turkey, pheasant or guinea fowl.

Makes about 900g/2lb

INGREDIENTS

900g/2lb/8 cups cranberries

450g/1lb sweet eating apples, washed and chopped with skins and cores intact

grated rind and juice of 1 orange

600ml/1 pint/2½ cups water

about 900g/2lb/4½ cups preserving or granulated sugar, warmed

COOK'S TIP

Do not be tempted to squeeze the jelly bag while it is draining or the jelly will become cloudy.

1 Put the cranberries and apples in a pan with the orange rind, juice and water. Bring to the boil then cover and simmer for 1 hour.

2 Remove the pan from the heat and set aside to cool slightly. Pour the fruit and juices into a scalded jelly bag suspended over a non-metallic bowl and leave to drain overnight.

3 Measure the strained juice into a preserving pan. Add 450g/1lb/ 2¼ cups sugar for every 600ml/ 1 pint/2½ cups strained juice.

4 Heat, stirring, over a low heat until the sugar has dissolved completely. Increase the heat and boil rapidly, without stirring, for 5–10 minutes, or until the jelly reaches setting point (105°C/220°F).

5 Remove the pan from the heat and skim off any scum from the surface using a slotted spoon. Ladle into warmed, sterilized jars, cover and seal. Leave to cool, then label and store in a cool, dark place.

red plum and cardamom jelly

The fragrance of warm, spicy cardamom combines wonderfully with all varieties of plum – red plums with a good tart flavour are perfect for making into this sweet, fruity, aromatic jelly. Serve it with plain rich ice creams and custards or spread it on toast for breakfast.

Makes about 1.8kg/4lb

INGREDIENTS

1.8kg/4lb red plums, stoned (pitted)

10ml/2 tsp crushed green cardamom pods

600ml/1 pint/2½ cups red grape juice

150ml/¼ pint/⅔ cup water

about 1.3kg/3lb/6½ cups preserving or granulated sugar, warmed

1 Put the plums, cardamom pods, grape juice and water in a large pan. Bring to the boil, then cover and simmer gently for 1 hour. Leave to cool slightly, then pour into a scalded jelly bag suspended over a non-metallic bowl and leave to drain overnight.

2 Measure the strained juice into a preserving pan. Add 450g/1lb/ 2¼ cups sugar for every 600ml/ 1 pint/2½ cups strained juice.

3 Heat the mixture over a low heat, stirring constantly until the sugar has dissolved completely. Increase the heat and boil, without stirring, for 10–15 minutes, or until the jelly reaches setting point (105°C/220°F).

4 Remove the pan from the heat and skim off any scum. Spoon the jelly into warmed sterilized jars, cover and seal. When cool, label and store in a cool, dark place.

rhubarb and mint jelly

This delicious jelly is very pretty, specked with tiny pieces of chopped fresh mint. It has a sharp, tangy flavour and is fabulous spread on toast or crumpets at tea time.

Makes about 2kg/4½lb

INGREDIENTS

1kg/2¼lb rhubarb

about 1.3kg/3lb/6½ cups preserving or granulated sugar, warmed

large bunch fresh mint

30ml/2 tbsp finely chopped fresh mint

COOK'S TIPS

- This recipe is a good way to use up older dark red or green-stemmed rhubarb, which is usually too tough to use for desserts.
- As well as serving as a delightful sweet preserve, this jelly is also very good served with fatty roast meats such as lamb and goose.

1 Using a sharp knife, cut the rhubarb into chunks and place in a large, heavy pan. Pour in just enough water to cover, cover the pan with a lid and cook until the rhubarb is soft.

2 Remove the pan from the heat and leave to cool slightly. Pour the stewed fruit and juices into a scalded jelly bag suspended over a non-metallic bowl and leave to drain overnight.

3 Measure the strained juice into a preserving pan and add 450g/1lb/2¼ cups warmed sugar for each 600ml/1 pint/2½ cups strained juice.

4 Add the bunch of mint to the pan. Bring to the boil, stirring until the sugar has dissolved. Boil to setting point (105°C/220°F). Remove the mint.

5 Leave to stand for 10 minutes, stir in the chopped mint, then pot and seal. Label when cold.

red gooseberry jelly

This delicious jelly is a wonderfully rich, dark red colour and has a deliciously tangy flavour – perfect for spreading on toast at any time of the day. Choose small dark red gooseberries to produce a jelly with the best colour and flavour.

Makes about 2kg/4½lb

INGREDIENTS

1.3kg/3lb/12 cups red gooseberries

2 red-skinned eating apples, washed and chopped with skins and cores intact

2.5cm/1in piece fresh root ginger, sliced

about 1.3kg/3lb/6½ cups preserving or granulated sugar, warmed

COOK'S TIPS

The amount of pectin in gooseberries diminishes as the fruit ripens so select firm, just ripe fruit when making this jelly to achieve a really good set.

1 Put the fruit and ginger in a large pan and add water to just below the level of the fruit. Cover and Simmer for 45 minutes.

2 Remove from the heat, cool slightly, then pour the fruit and juices into a scalded jelly bag suspended over a non-metallic bowl and leave to drain overnight.

3 Measure the strained juice into a preserving pan and add 450g/1lb/2¼ cups warmed sugar for every 600ml/1 pint/2½ cups juice.

4 Stir over a low heat until the sugar has dissolved. Boil for about 10 minutes, or to setting point (105°C/220°F). Skim off any scum, then pot, seal and label.

rosehip and apple jelly

This economical jelly is made with windfall apples and wild rosehips. It is rich in vitamin C, full of flavour, and excellent spread on freshly toasted crumpets or scones.

Makes about 2kg/4½lb

INGREDIENTS

1kg/2¼lb windfall apples, peeled, trimmed and quartered

450g/1lb firm, ripe rosehips

about 1.3kg/3lb/6½ cups preserving or granulated sugar, warmed

1 Place the quartered apples in a large pan with just enough water to cover, plus 300ml/½ pint/ 1¼ cups of extra water.

COOK'S TIP

There is no need to remove all the peel from the apples: simply cut out any bruised, damaged or bad areas.

2 Bring the mixture to the boil and cook gently until the apples soften and turn to a pulp. Meanwhile, chop the rosehips coarsely. Add the rosehips to the pan with the apple and simmer for 10 minutes.

3 Remove from the heat and stand for 10 minutes, then pour the mixture into a scalded jelly bag suspended over a non-metallic bowl and leave to drain overnight.

4 Measure the juice into a preserving pan and bring to the boil. Add 400g/14oz/2 cups warmed sugar for each 600ml/ 1 pint/2½ cups of liquid. Stir until the sugar has completely dissolved. Boil to setting point (105°C/220°F).

5 Pour the jelly into warmed, sterilized jars and seal. Label and store when completely cold.

spiced cider and apple jelly

This wonderful spicy jelly has a rich, warming flavour, making it ideal to serve during the cold winter months. Serve as a spread or use it to sweeten apple pies and desserts.

Makes about 1.3kg/3lb

INGREDIENTS

900g/2lb cooking apples, coarsely chopped with skins and cores intact

900ml/1¼ pints/3¾ cups sweet (hard) cider

juice and pips (seeds) of 2 oranges

1 cinnamon stick

6 whole cloves

150ml/¼ pint/⅔ cup water

about 900g/2lb/4½ cups preserving or granulated sugar, warmed

1 Put the apples, cider, juice and pips, cinnamon, cloves and water in a large pan. Bring to the boil, cover and simmer for about 1 hour.

2 Leave to cool slightly, then pour the fruit into a scalded jelly bag suspended over a non-metallic bowl and leave to drain overnight.

3 Measure the strained juice into a preserving pan. Add 450g/1lb/ 2¼ cups warmed sugar for every 600ml/1 pint/2½ cups juice.

4 Heat, stirring, over a low heat until the sugar has dissolved. Increase the heat and boil, without stirring, for 10 minutes, or until the jelly reaches setting point (105°C/220°F).

5 Remove from the heat and skim off any scum. Ladle into warmed sterilized jars. Cover, seal and label.

sweet fruit jellies • 53

quince and coriander jelly

When raw, quinces are inedible but once cooked and sweetened they become aromatic and have a wonderful flavour, which is enhanced here by the addition of warm, spicy coriander seeds.

Makes about 900g/2lb

INGREDIENTS

1kg/2¼lb quinces, washed and coarsely chopped with skins and cores intact

15ml/1 tbsp coriander seeds

juice and pips (seeds) of 2 large lemons

900ml/1½ pints/3¾ cups water

about 900g/2lb/4½ cups preserving or granulated sugar, warmed

VARIATION

If you don't have enough quinces, you can make up the quantity with apples. The flavour won't be quite the same but the jelly will still be delicious.

1 Put the quinces in a pan with the coriander seeds, lemon juice and pips, and the water. Bring to the boil, cover and simmer gently for about 1½ hours.

2 Leave the fruit to cool slightly, then pour into a scalded jelly bag suspended over a non-metallic bowl and leave to drain overnight.

3 Measure the strained juice into a preserving pan. Add 450g/1lb/ 2¼ cups warmed sugar for every 600ml/1 pint/2½ cups juice.

4 Heat, stirring, over a low heat until the sugar has completely dissolved. Increase the heat and boil rapidly, without stirring, for 5–10 minutes or until the jelly reaches setting point (105°C/220°F).

5 Remove the pan from the heat and skim off any scum from the surface using a slotted spoon. Ladle into warmed sterilized jars, cover and seal. When cold, label and store in a cool, dark place.

COOK'S TIP

Jellies can look very pretty served in decorative glasses. Bottle the jelly in jars as above, then, when ready to serve, gently heat the jelly in a pan with a very small amount of water until melted. Pour the jelly into a heatproof glass and leave to set before serving.

scented geranium and pear jelly

This jelly uses the leaves of scented geranium to give an aromatic lift to the pears. Use rose-scented leaves if you have them, otherwise add a couple of drops of rose water to the strained juice.

Makes about 900g/2lb

INGREDIENTS

900g/2lb Comice pears, washed and coarsely chopped with skins and cores intact

7 rose-scented geranium leaves, plus extra for storing

juice and pips (seeds) of 1 lemon

60ml/4 tbsp clear honey

900ml/1½ pints/3¾ cups water

about 900g/2lb/4½ cups preserving or granulated sugar, warmed

1 Put the pears, geranium leaves, lemon juice, honey and water in a large pan. Bring to the boil, then cover and simmer for 1 hour.

2 Remove the pan from the heat and leave to cool slightly. Pour the fruit into a scalded jelly bag suspended over a non-metallic bowl and leave to drain overnight.

3 Measure the strained juice into a preserving pan. Add 450g/1lb/2¼ cups warmed sugar for every 600ml/1 pint/2½ cups juice.

4 Heat, stirring, over a low heat until the sugar has dissolved. Increase the heat and boil rapidly, without stirring, for 10 minutes, or to setting point (105°C/220°F).

5 Remove the pan from the heat and skim off any scum using a slotted spoon. Place a blanched geranium leaf into each warmed sterilized jar, then ladle in the jelly. Cover and seal, then label.

sweet fruit jellies • 55

pineapple and passion fruit jelly

This exotic jelly has a wonderful warming glow to its taste and appearance. For the best-flavoured jelly, use a tart-tasting, not too ripe pineapple rather than a very ripe, sweet one.

Makes about 900g/2lb

INGREDIENTS

1 large pineapple, peeled, topped and tailed and coarsely chopped

4 passion fruit, halved, with seeds and pulp scooped out

900ml/1½ pints/3¾ cups water

about 900g/2lb/4½ cups preserving or granulated sugar, warmed

COOK'S TIP

For the best flavour, choose passion fruits with dark, wrinkled skins.

1 Place the pineapple and the passion fruit seeds and pulp in a large pan with the water.

2 Bring the mixture to the boil, cover and simmer for 1½ hours. Remove from the heat and leave to cool slightly. Transfer the fruit to a food processor and process briefly.

3 Pour the fruit pulp and any juices from the pan, into a scalded jelly bag suspended over a non-metallic bowl and leave to drain overnight.

4 Measure the strained juice into a preserving pan and add 450g/1lb/2¼ cups warmed sugar for every 600ml/1 pint/2½ cups juice.

5 Heat gently, stirring, until the sugar has dissolved. Increase the heat and boil rapidly, without stirring, for 10–15 minutes or to setting point (105°C/220°F).

6 Remove the pan from the heat and skim off any scum using a slotted spoon. Ladle the jelly into warmed sterilized jars, cover and seal. When cool, label and store in a cool, dark place.

sweet fruit jellies

pomegranate and grenadine jelly

The slightly tart flavoured, jewel-like flesh of the pomegranate makes the most wonderful jelly. Be careful though, because pomegranate juice can stain indelibly when spilt on clothing.

Makes about 900g/2lb

INGREDIENTS

6 ripe red pomegranates, peeled and seeds removed from membranes

120ml/4fl oz/½ cup grenadine syrup

juice and pips (seeds) of 2 oranges

300ml/½ pint/1¼ cups water

about 900g/2lb/4½ cups preserving or granulated sugar, warmed

1 Put the pomegranate seeds in bowl and crush to release their juice. Transfer them to a pan and add the grenadine, orange juice, pips and water.

2 Bring the mixture to the boil, cover and simmer for 1½ hours. Mash the fruit and leave to cool slightly, then pour into a scalded jelly bag suspended over a bowl and leave to drain overnight.

3 Measure the juice into a pan and add 450g/1lb/2¼ cups sugar for every 600ml/1 pint/2½ cups juice.

4 Heat, stirring, over a low heat until the sugar has dissolved. Increase the heat and boil rapidly, without stirring, for 5–10 minutes, or until the jelly reaches setting point (105°C/220°F).

5 Remove the pan from the heat and skim off any scum. Ladle into warmed sterilized jars, cover, seal and label. Store in a cool place.

marmalades

These classic preserves come somewhere between a jam and a jelly and are traditionally served for breakfast. Usually made of citrus fruits, marmalades have a jelly base with small pieces of fruit suspended in it. They can be tart and bitter with thick-cut shreds of peel, or sweet with thinly cut zest. The Seville orange is favoured because of its refreshing tang and high pectin content but any citrus fruit can be used, as long as its shredded rind is cooked until very tender. All the recipes in this chapter will keep for at least 1 year.

oxford marmalade

The characteristic caramel colour and rich flavour of a traditional Oxford marmalade is obtained by cutting the fruit coarsely and cooking it for several hours before adding the sugar.

Makes about 2.25kg/5lb

INGREDIENTS
900g/2lb Seville (Temple) oranges
1.75 litres/3 pints/7½ cups water
1.3kg/3lb/6½ cups granulated sugar, warmed

COOK'S TIP
Traditionalists say that only bitter oranges such as Seville should be used to make marmalade. Although this isn't always true, it is most certainly the case when making Oxford marmalade.

1 Scrub the orange skins, then remove the rind using a vegetable peeler. Thickly slice the rind and put in a large pan.

2 Chop the fruit, reserving the pips (seeds), and add to the rind in the pan, along with the water. Tie the orange pips in a piece of muslin (cheesecloth) and add to the pan. Bring to the boil, then cover and simmer for 2 hours. Add more water during cooking to maintain the same volume. Remove the pan from the heat and leave overnight.

3 The next day, remove the muslin bag from the oranges, squeezing well, and return the pan to the heat. Bring to the boil, then cover and simmer for 1 hour.

4 Add the warmed sugar to the pan, then slowly bring the mixture to the boil, stirring until the sugar has dissolved completely. Increase the heat and boil rapidly for about 15 minutes, or until setting point is reached (105°C/220°F).

5 Remove the pan from the heat and skim off any scum from the surface. Leave to cool for about 5 minutes, stir, then pour into warmed sterilized jars and seal. When cold, label, then store in a cool, dark place.

st clement's marmalade

This classic preserve made from oranges and lemons has a lovely citrus tang. It has a light, refreshing flavour and is perfect for serving for breakfast, spread on freshly toasted bread.

Makes about 2.25kg/5lb

INGREDIENTS

450g/1lb Seville (Temple) oranges
450g/1lb sweet oranges
4 lemons
1.5 litres/2½ pints/6¼ cups water
1.2kg/2½lb/5½ cups granulated sugar, warmed

1 Wash the oranges and lemons, then halve and squeeze the juice into a large pan. Tie the pips (seeds) and membranes in a muslin (cheesecloth) bag, shred the orange and lemon rind and add to the pan.

2 Add the water to the pan, bring to the boil, then cover and simmer for 2 hours. Remove the muslin bag, leave to cool, then squeeze any liquid back into the pan.

3 Add the warmed sugar to the pan and stir over a low heat until completely dissolved. Bring to the boil and boil rapidly for about 15 minutes or until the marmalade reaches setting point (105°C/220°F).

4 Remove the pan from the heat and skim off any scum from the surface. Leave to cool for about 5 minutes, stir, then pour into warmed sterilized jars and seal. When cold, label, then store in a cool, dark place.

pink grapefruit and cranberry marmalade

Cranberries give this glorious marmalade an extra tartness and a full fruit flavour, as well as an inimitable vibrant colour. The resulting preserve makes a lively choice for breakfast or a brilliant accompaniment for cold roast turkey during the festive season.

Makes about 2.25kg/5lb

INGREDIENTS

675g/1½lb pink grapefruit
juice and pips (seeds) of 2 lemons
900ml/1½ pints/3¾ cups water
225g/8oz/2 cups cranberries
1.3kg/3lb/6½ cups granulated sugar, warmed

COOK'S TIP

You can use fresh or frozen cranberries to make this marmalade. Either gives equally good results.

1 Wash, halve and quarter the grapefruit, then slice them thinly, reserving the pips (seeds) and any juice that runs out.

2 Tie the grapefruit and lemon pips in a muslin (cheesecloth) bag and place in a large pan with the grapefruit slices and lemon juice.

3 Add the water and bring to the boil. Cover and simmer gently for 1½–2 hours, or until the grapefruit rind is very tender. Remove the muslin bag, leave to cool, then squeeze over the pan.

4 Add the cranberries to the pan, then bring to the boil. Simmer for 15–20 minutes, or until the berries have popped and softened.

5 Add the sugar to the pan and stir over a low heat until the sugar has completely dissolved. Bring to the boil and boil rapidly for about 10 minutes, or until setting point is reached (105°C/220°F).

6 Remove the pan from the heat and skim off any scum from the surface using a slotted spoon. Leave to cool for 5–10 minutes, then stir and pour into warmed sterilized jars. Seal, then label when the marmalade is cold.

ruby red grapefruit marmalade

If you prefer a really tangy marmalade, grapefruit is the perfect choice. To achieve a wonderfully red-blushed preserve, look for the red variety rather than pink. They have a wonderful flavour and make a really delicious, sweet, jewel-coloured preserve.

Makes about 1.8kg/4lb

INGREDIENTS
- 900g/2lb ruby red grapefruit
- 1 lemon
- 1.2 litres/2 pints/5 cups water
- 1.3kg/3lb/6½ cups granulated sugar, warmed

1 Wash the grapefruit and lemon and remove the rind in thick pieces using a vegetable peeler. Cut the fruit in half and squeeze the juice into a preserving pan, reserving all the pips (seeds).

2 Put the pips and membranes from the fruit in a muslin (cheesecloth) bag and add to the pan. Discard the grapefruit and lemon shells.

3 Using a sharp knife, cut the grapefruit and lemon rind into thin or coarse shreds, as preferred, and place in the pan.

COOK'S TIP
Although you can use yellow grapefruit to make this marmalade, it tends to give a very pale result with more tang than the ruby red variety, but a much less fruity flavour.

4 Add the water to the pan and bring to the boil. Cover and simmer for 2 hours, or until the rind is very tender.

5 Remove the muslin bag from the pan, leave to cool, then squeeze it over the pan. Add the sugar and stir over a low heat until it has dissolved. Bring to the boil, then boil rapidly for 10–15 minutes, or to setting point (105°C/220°F).

6 Remove the pan from the heat and skim off any scum using a slotted spoon. Leave to cool for about 10 minutes, then stir and pour into warmed sterilized jars. Seal, then label when cold.

marmalades • 63

lemon and ginger marmalade

This combination of lemon and ginger produces a really zesty and versatile preserve, perfect served on toast at any time of day. It is also excellent added to meat glazes. Mix a few spoonfuls of the marmalade with a little soy sauce and brush over meat before grilling.

Makes about 1.8kg/4lb

INGREDIENTS

1.2kg/2½lb lemons

150g/5oz fresh root ginger, peeled and finely grated

1.2 litres/2 pints/5 cups water

900g/2lb/4½ cups granulated sugar, warmed

COOK'S TIP

When choosing fresh root ginger, select young, firm, fine-skinned pieces. For the best results, grate only the tender, juicy parts of the root and discard any tough, hairy parts.

1 Quarter and slice the lemons. Tie the pips (seeds) in a muslin (cheesecloth) bag and place in a preserving pan with the lemons, ginger and water. Bring to the boil, cover with a lid and simmer for 2 hours, or until the fruit is tender.

2 Remove the muslin bag from the pan, leave to cool then squeeze over the pan to release all the juice and pectin. Stir in the sugar over a low heat until dissolved, then increase the heat and boil for 5–10 minutes, or until setting point is reached (105°C/220°F).

3 Remove the pan from the heat and skim off any scum from the surface using a slotted spoon.

4 Leave to cool for 5 minutes, stir, then pour into warmed sterilized jars and seal. When cold, label and store in a cool place.

orange and coriander marmalade

This traditional marmalade made with bitter Seville oranges has the added zing of warm, spicy coriander. Cut the orange rind into thin or coarse shreds, according to taste.

Makes about 1.8kg/4lb

INGREDIENTS

675g/1½lb Seville (Temple) oranges

2 lemons

15ml/1 tbsp crushed coriander seeds

1.5 litres/2½ pints/6¼ cups water

900g/2lb/4½ cups granulated sugar, warmed

1 Cut the oranges and lemons in half and squeeze out all the juice. Place the orange and lemon pips (seeds) in a muslin (cheesecloth) bag. Using a sharp knife, cut the rind into shreds and place in a preserving pan with the juice.

2 Put the coriander seeds in the muslin bag with the pips and place in the pan. Add the water and bring to the boil. Cover and simmer for 2 hours, or until the mixture has reduced by half and the peel is soft.

3 Remove the muslin bag from the pan. Set it aside to cool, then squeeze it over the pan to release all the juices and pectin.

4 Add the sugar to the pan and stir over a low heat until it has dissolved. Bring to the boil and boil rapidly for 5–10 minutes, or to setting point (105°C/220°F).

5 Remove the pan from the heat and skim off any scum from the surface using a slotted spoon. Leave to cool for 5 minutes, stir then pour into warmed sterilized jars. Seal, then label when cold.

marmalades • 65

spiced pumpkin marmalade

The bright orange colour and warm flavour of this marmalade is guaranteed to banish the winter blues. The addition of pumpkin gives the preserve more body and a lovely, satisfying texture. It's perfect for spreading on hot buttered toast or serving with warm croissants.

Makes about 2.75kg/6lb

INGREDIENTS

- 900g/2lb Seville (Temple) oranges, washed and halved
- 450g/1lb lemons, halved and thinly sliced, pips (seeds) reserved
- 2 cinnamon sticks
- 2.5cm/1in piece fresh root ginger, peeled and thinly sliced
- 1.5ml/¼ tsp grated nutmeg
- 1.75 litres/3 pints/7½ cups water
- 800g/1¾lb squash or pumpkin, peeled, seeds (pips) removed and thinly sliced
- 1.3kg/3lb/6½ cups granulated sugar, warmed

1 Squeeze the juice from the oranges and pour into a preserving pan. Remove the white membranes and reserve with the pips.

2 Thinly slice the orange rind and place in the pan, along with the sliced lemons. Tie the orange and lemon pips and membranes in a muslin (cheesecloth) bag with the spices and add to the pan with the water. Bring to the boil, then cover and simmer for 1 hour.

3 Add the pumpkin to the pan and continue cooking for 1–1½ hours. Remove the muslin bag, leave to cool, then squeeze over the pan.

4 Stir in the sugar over a low heat until completely dissolved. Bring to the boil, then boil rapidly for 15 minutes, or until the marmalade becomes thick and reaches setting point (105°C/220°F). Stir once or twice to ensure the marmalade does not stick to the pan.

5 Remove the pan from the heat and skim off any scum. Leave to cool for 5 minutes, then stir and pour into warmed sterilized jars. Cover the surface of the preserve with wax discs, then seal. Label when the marmalade is cold and store in a cool, dark place.

clementine and liqueur marmalade

Small, tart clementines make a particularly full-flavoured preserve, which can be put to a wide variety of culinary uses. Stir it into yogurt or warm it with a little water to make a zesty sauce for pancakes or crêpes. It is also superlative served with smooth ripe Brie and crisp crackers.

Makes about 1.8kg/4lb

INGREDIENTS

900g/2lb clementines, washed and halved

juice and pips (seeds) of 2 lemons

900ml/1½ pints/3¾ cups water

900g/2lb/4½ cups granulated sugar, warmed

60ml/4 tbsp Grand Marnier or Cointreau

COOK'S TIP

Any member of the mandarin family can be used to make this preserve, but clementines give the best result.

1 Slice the clementines, reserving any pips. Tie the pips in a muslin (cheesecloth) bag with the lemon pips and place in a large pan with the sliced fruit.

2 Add the lemon juice and water to the pan and bring to the boil, then cover and simmer for about 1½ hours, or until the rind is very tender. Remove the muslin bag, cool, then squeeze over the pan.

3 Stir in the sugar over a low heat until dissolved, then bring to the boil and cook 5–10 minutes, or to setting point (105°C/220°F).

4 Remove the pan from the heat and skim off any scum. Cool for 5 minutes, then stir in the liqueur and pour into warmed sterilized jars. Seal, then label when cold.

peach and kumquat marmalade

Combined with sweet, scented peaches, kumquats make a wonderful, fresh-tasting preserve. This lovely marmalade has a jam-like consistency and is great at any time of day.

Makes about 1.8kg/4lb

INGREDIENTS

675g/1½lb kumquats, sliced thinly, pips (seeds) and juice reserved

juice and pips of 1 lime

900g/2lb peaches, skinned and thinly sliced, skins reserved

900ml/1½ pints/3¾ cups water

900g/2lb/4½ cups granulated sugar, warmed

1 Tie the pips and the peach skins in a muslin (cheesecloth) bag and put in a pan with the kumquats, juices and water. Bring to the boil, then cover and simmer for 50 minutes.

2 Add the peaches to the pan, bring to the boil, then simmer for 40–50 minutes, or until the fruit has become very soft. Remove the muslin bag, leave to cool, then squeeze over the pan.

3 Add the sugar to the pan and stir over a low heat until it has dissolved. Bring the mixture to the boil, then boil rapidly for about 15 minutes, stirring occasionally, to setting point (105°C/220°F).

4 Remove the pan from the heat and skim off any scum from the surface using a slotted spoon.

5 Leave to cool for 5–10 minutes, then stir and pour into warmed sterilized jars. Seal, then label when the jars are cold. Store in a cool, dark place.

apricot and orange marmalade

Serve this sweet marmalade with warm croissants and strong coffee for a leisurely weekend breakfast. The combination of oranges and rich-tasting apricots is a winner.

Makes about 1.5kg/3lb 6oz

INGREDIENTS

2 Seville (Temple) oranges, washed and quartered

1 lemon, washed and quartered

1.2 litres/2 pints/5 cups water

900g/2lb apricots, stoned (pitted) and thinly sliced

900g/2lb/4½ cups granulated sugar, warmed

COOK'S TIP

It is important to use a food processor to chop the oranges and lemon for this recipe. Chopping them this finely gives the marmalade its wonderful consistency. Preparing the fruits by hand will not give the same result.

1 Remove the pips (seeds) from the citrus fruit and tie in a muslin (cheesecloth) bag. Finely chop the oranges and lemons in a food processor and put in a large pan with the muslin bag and water.

2 Bring the mixture to the boil, then simmer, covered, for 1 hour.

3 Add the apricots to the pan, bring to the boil, then simmer for 30–40 minutes, or until the fruits are very tender.

4 Add the sugar to the pan and stir over a low heat until the sugar has dissolved. Bring to the boil, then boil rapidly for 15 minutes, stirring occasionally, until setting point is reached (105°C/220°F).

5 Remove the pan from the heat and skim off any scum from the surface using a slotted spoon. Leave to cool for about 5 minutes, then stir and pour into warmed sterilized jars. Seal, then label when cold. Store in a cool place.

curds, butters and cheeses

These smooth, thick, luscious preserves capture the colours and flavours of the season. Butters and curds are thick and spreadable, delicious spooned on to toast or griddle cakes. In contrast, cheeses are firmer and can be cut into wedges or slices, or set in small individual moulds. Serve them as a delicious accompaniment to roast meats or dairy cheeses, or cut into wedges, dredge in sugar and serve as a sweetmeat after the meal.

lemon curd

This classic tangy, creamy curd is still one of the most popular of all the curds. It is delicious spread thickly over freshly baked white bread or served with American-style pancakes, and also makes a wonderfully rich, zesty sauce spooned over fresh fruit tarts.

Makes about 450g/1lb

INGREDIENTS

3 lemons

200g/7oz/1 cup caster (superfine) sugar

115g/4oz/8 tbsp unsalted (sweet) butter, diced

2 large (US extra large) eggs

2 large (US extra large) egg yolks

1 Wash the lemons, then finely grate the rind and place in a large heatproof bowl. Using a sharp knife, halve the lemons and squeeze the juice into the bowl. Set over a pan of gently simmering water and add the sugar and butter. Stir until the sugar has dissolved and the butter melted.

2 Put the eggs and yolks in a bowl and beat together with a fork. Pour the eggs through a sieve (strainer) into the lemon mixture, and whisk well until thoroughly combined.

3 Stir the mixture constantly over the heat until the lemon curd thickens and lightly coats the back of a wooden spoon.

4 Remove the pan from the heat and pour the curd into small, warmed sterilized jars. Cover, seal and label. Store in a cool, dark place, ideally in the refrigerator. Use within 3 months. (Once opened, store in the refrigerator.)

COOK'S TIP

If you are really impatient when it comes to cooking, it is possible to cook the curd in a heavy pan directly over a low heat. However, you really need to watch it like a hawk to avoid the mixture curdling. If the curd looks as though it's beginning to curdle, plunge the base of the pan in cold water and beat vigorously.

curds, butters and cheeses

Seville orange curd

Using flavoursome Seville oranges gives this curd a fantastic orange flavour and a real citrus tang. It is perfect for spreading on toast for breakfast or at tea time, and is also superlative folded into whipped cream and used as a filling for cakes, roulades and scones.

Makes about 450g/1lb

INGREDIENTS
2 Seville (Temple) oranges
115g/4oz/8 tbsp unsalted (sweet) butter, diced
200g/7oz/1 cup caster (superfine) sugar
2 large (US extra large) eggs
2 large (US extra large) egg yolks

1 Wash the oranges, then finely grate the rind and place in a large heatproof bowl. Halve the oranges and squeeze the juice into the bowl with the rind.

2 Place the bowl over a pan of gently simmering water and add the butter and sugar. Stir until the sugar has completely dissolved and the butter melted.

3 Put the eggs and yolks in a small bowl and lightly whisk, then pour into the orange mixture through a sieve. Whisk them together until thoroughly combined.

4 Stir the orange and egg mixture constantly over the heat until the mixture thickens and lightly coats the back of a wooden spoon.

5 Pour the orange curd into small, warmed sterilized jars, cover and seal. Store in a cool, dark place, preferably in the refrigerator.

WATCHPOINTS
• The very young, the elderly, pregnant women, and those with a compromised immune system are advised against eating raw eggs or food containing raw eggs. Although the eggs in fruit curds are lightly cooked, they may still be unsuitable for these groups of people.
• Fruit curds do not have the shelf-life of many other preserves and should be used within 3 months of making.
• Once opened, always store fruit curds in the refrigerator.

grapefruit curd

If you favour tangy and refreshing preserves, this grapefruit curd is the one to try. Really fresh free-range eggs give the best results and flavour when making curd.

Makes about 675g/1½lb

INGREDIENTS

finely grated rind and juice of 1 grapefruit

115g/4oz/8 tbsp unsalted (sweet) butter, diced

200g/7oz/1 cup caster (superfine) sugar

4 large (US extra large) eggs, lightly beaten

1 Put the grapefruit rind and juice in a large heatproof bowl with the butter and sugar, and set over a pan of gently simmering water. Heat the mixture, stirring occasionally, until the sugar has dissolved and the butter melted.

2 Add the beaten eggs to the fruit mixture, straining them through a sieve (strainer). Whisk together, then stir constantly over the heat until the mixture thickens and lightly coats the back of a wooden spoon.

3 Pour the curd into small, warmed sterilized jars, cover and seal. Label when the jars are cold. Store in a cool, dark place, preferably in the refrigerator and use within 3 months. (Once opened, store the curd in the refrigerator.)

VARIATION

Tangy grapefruit and sweet orange marry particularly well in creamy fruit curds. Add the grated rind of a small orange to this grapefruit recipe for an extra zingy, zesty alternative.

passion fruit curd

The tropical flavour and aroma of passion fruit fills this curd with a gloriously sunny character. It is perfect spread on toasted English muffins or little American pancakes.

Makes about 675g/1½lb

INGREDIENTS
- grated rind and juice of 2 lemons
- 115g/4oz/8 tbsp unsalted (sweet) butter, diced
- 275g/10oz/1⅓ cups caster (superfine) sugar
- 4 passion fruit
- 4 eggs
- 2 egg yolks

1 Place the lemon rind and juice in a large heatproof bowl and add the butter and sugar.

2 Halve the passion fruit and scoop the seeds into a sieve (strainer) set over the bowl. Press out all the juice and discard the seeds.

3 Place the bowl over a pan of gently simmering water and stir occasionally until the sugar has dissolved and the butter melted.

4 Beat the eggs and yolks together and add to the bowl, pouring them through a sieve, then whisk well to combine. Stir constantly until the mixture thickens and lightly coats the back of a spoon.

5 Pour the curd into small, warmed sterilized jars, cover and seal. Store in a cool, dark place, preferably in the refrigerator and use within 3 months. (Once opened, store in the refrigerator.)

apple and cinnamon butter

Fans of apple pies and crumbles will love this luscious apple butter. Serve on toast or with warmed brioche for a breakfast treat or with pancakes and cream for tea.

Makes about 1.8kg/4lb

INGREDIENTS

475ml/16fl oz/2 cups dry (hard) cider

450g/1lb tart cooking apples, peeled, cored and sliced

450g/1lb eating apples, peeled, cored and sliced

grated rind and juice of 1 lemon

675g/1½lb/scant 3½ cups granulated sugar, warmed

5ml/1 tsp ground cinnamon

COOK'S TIP

Leaving the butter to stand for 2 days give the flavours a chance to develop.

1 Pour the cider into a large pan and bring to the boil. Boil hard until the volume is reduced by half, then add the apples and lemon rind and juice.

2 Cover the pan and cook for 10 minutes. Uncover and continue cooking for 20–30 minutes, or until the apples are very soft.

3 Leave the mixture to cool slightly, then pour into a food processor or blender and blend to a purée. Press through a fine sieve (strainer) into a bowl.

4 Measure the purée into a large heavy pan, adding 275g/10oz/1⅓ cups warmed sugar for every 600ml/1 pint/2½ cups of purée. Add the ground cinnamon and stir well to combine.

5 Gently heat the mixture, stirring continuously, until the sugar has completely dissolved. Increase the heat and boil steadily for about 20 minutes, stirring frequently, until the mixture forms a thick purée that hold its shape when spooned on to a cold plate.

6 Spoon the apple and cinnamon butter into warmed sterilized jars. Seal and label, then store in a cool, dark place for 2 days to allow the flavours to develop before serving.

pear and vanilla butter

The delicate flavour of pears is enhanced by vanilla in this butter that really captures the essence of the fruit. It is well worth allowing it to mature for a few days before eating.

Makes about 675g/1½lb

INGREDIENTS

900g/2lb pears, peeled, cored and chopped

juice of 3 lemons

300ml/½ pint/1¼ cups water

1 vanilla pod (bean), split

675g/1½lb/scant 3½ cups granulated sugar, warmed

1 Place the pears in a large pan with the lemon juice, water and vanilla pod. Bring to the boil, then cover and simmer for 10 minutes. Uncover the pan and continue cooking for a further 15–20 minutes, or until the pears are very soft.

2 Remove the vanilla pod from the pan, then carefully scrape the seeds into the fruit mixture using the tip of a knife.

3 Tip the fruit and juices into a food processor or blender and blend to a purée. Press the purée through a fine sieve (strainer) into a bowl.

4 Measure the purée into a large heavy pan, adding 275g/10oz/ 1⅓ cups warmed sugar for every 600ml/1 pint/2½ cups of purée.

5 Stir the mixture over a low heat until the sugar dissolves. Increase the heat and boil for 15 minutes, stirring, until the mixture forms a thick purée that holds its shape when spooned on to a cold plate.

6 Spoon the pear butter into small, warmed sterilized jars. Seal, label and store in a cool, dark place for at least 2 days before serving.

COOK'S TIPS

• Fruit butters have a soft spreading consistency – thicker than fruit curds, but softer than fruit cheeses. They make an excellent tea time preserve.

• Fruit butters keep well in sealed jars and can be stored for up to 3 months. Once opened, they should be stored in the refrigerator.

pumpkin and maple butter

This all-American butter has a lovely bright, autumnal colour and flavour. It is perfect served spread on little pancakes fresh from the griddle, or used as a filling or topping for cakes.

Makes about 675g/1½lb

INGREDIENTS

1.2kg/2½lb pumpkin or butternut squash, peeled, seeded and chopped
450ml/¾ pint/scant 2 cups water
grated rind and juice of 1 orange
5ml/1 tsp ground cinnamon
120ml/4fl oz/½ cup maple syrup
675g/1½lb/scant 3½ cups granulated sugar, warmed

VARIATION

This butter is also delicious made with clear honey instead of maple syrup. It adds a distinctive flavour.

1 Put the pumpkin or squash in the pan with the water and cook for 30–40 minutes, or until it is very tender. Drain and, using the back of a spoon, press the cooked pumpkin or squash through a fine sieve into a bowl.

2 Stir the orange rind and juice, cinnamon and maple syrup into the purée, then measure the purée into a large pan, adding 275g/ 10oz/1⅓ cups warmed sugar for every 600ml/1 pint/2½ cups purée.

3 Gently heat the purée, stirring, until the sugar has dissolved. Increase the heat and boil for 10–20 minutes, stirring frequently, until the mixture forms a thick purée that holds its shape when spooned on to a cold plate.

4 Spoon the butter into small, warmed sterilized jars. Seal and label, then store in a cool, dark place for 2 days before eating.

mango and cardamom butter

You need to use really ripe mangoes for this recipe. If the mangoes are not ripe enough, they will need much longer cooking and will not produce such a richly flavoured butter.

Makes about 675g/1½lb

INGREDIENTS

900g/2lb ripe mangoes, peeled

6 green cardamom pods, split

120ml/4fl oz/½ cup freshly squeezed lemon juice

120ml/4fl oz/½ cup freshly squeezed orange juice

50ml/2fl oz/¼ cup water

675g/1½lb/scant 3½ cups granulated sugar, warmed

1 Cut the mango flesh away from the stones and chop, then place it in a pan with the cardamom pods, fruit juices and water.

2 Cover and simmer for 10 minutes. Remove the lid and simmer for a further 25 minutes, or until the mangoes are very soft and there is very little liquid left in the pan.

3 Remove the cardamom pods from the pan and discard. Transfer the fruit to a food processor and blend to a purée. Press the purée through a fine sieve (strainer) into a bowl.

4 Measure the purée into a large, heavy pan, adding 275g/10oz/ 1⅓ cups warmed sugar for every 600ml/1 pint/2½ cups purée. Gently heat, stirring, until the sugar has dissolved. Increase the heat and boil for 10–20 minutes, stirring, until a thick butter forms that holds its shape when spooned on to a cold plate.

5 Spoon the mango and cardamom butter into small, warmed sterilized jars. Seal and label, then store in a cool, dark place for at least 2 days before eating. (The butter can be stored for up to 3 months.)

damson and vanilla cheese

You can use any type or variety of plum for this cheese, but damsons have the most intense flavour. This cheese is good with roast lamb, duck and game, or semi-soft cheese.

Makes about 900g/2lb

INGREDIENTS

1.5kg/3lb 6oz damsons
1 vanilla pod (bean), split
800g/1¾lb/4 cups granulated sugar, warmed

COOK'S TIPS

• When the cheese is ready, you should be able to see the base of the pan when a wooden spoon is drawn through the mixture. To test the set, spoon a small amount of the damson mixture on to a chilled plate; it should form a firm jelly.
• To make cheese shapes, spoon the mixture into greased moulds, and leave to set before turning out and serving.

1 Wash the damsons and place in a large pan with the vanilla pod and pour in enough water to come halfway up the fruit. Cover and simmer for 30 minutes.

2 Remove the vanilla pod from the pan and scrape the seeds back into the pan using the point of a knife.

3 Press the fruit and juices through a sieve (strainer) into a bowl. Measure the purée into a large, heavy pan, adding 400g/14oz/2 cups sugar for every 600ml/1 pint/2½ cups purée.

4 Gently heat the purée, stirring, until the sugar has dissolved. Increase the heat slightly and cook for about 45 minutes, stirring frequently with a wooden spoon, until very thick.

5 Spoon the damson cheese into warmed, sterilized jars. Seal and label, then store in a cool, dark place for 2–3 months to dry out slightly before eating.

quince cheese

This wonderfully fragrant fruit cheese is particularly good set in squares, dusted with sugar and served as a sweetmeat, but it is just as good bottled in jars and spooned out as required.

Makes about 900g/2lb

INGREDIENTS

1.3kg/3lb quinces
800g/1¾lb/4 cups granulated sugar, warmed
caster (superfine) sugar, for dusting

COOK'S TIP

Rather than setting the cheese and cutting it into squares, simply spoon the mixture into warmed, sterilized, straight-sided jars. Seal and label, then store in a cool, dark place for 2–3 months to dry out slightly before eating.

1 Wash the quinces, then chop and place in a large pan. Pour in enough water to nearly cover the fruit, then cover with a lid and simmer for 45 minutes, or until the fruit is very tender. Cool slightly.

2 Press the mixture through a fine sieve into a bowl. Measure the purée into a large, heavy pan, adding 400g/14oz/2 cups sugar for every 600ml/1 pint/2½ cups purée. Heat gently, stirring, until the sugar has dissolved. Increase the heat and cook for 40–50 minutes, stirring frequently, until very thick (see Cook's Tip, left).

3 Pour the mixture into a small oiled baking tin (pan) and leave to set for 24 hours. Cut into small squares, dust with sugar and store in an airtight container.

spiced cherry cheese

For the best results, try to use cherries that have a good tart flavour and dark red flesh. Serve as an accompaniment to strong cheese, or sliced with roast duck or pork.

Makes about 900g/2lb

INGREDIENTS

1.5kg/3lb 6oz/8¼ cups cherries, stoned (pitted)
2 cinnamon sticks
800g/1¾lb/4 cups granulated sugar, warmed

COOK'S TIPS

• Store the cheese in a cool, dark place for 2–3 months before eating.
• To serve a fruit cheese in slices, turn it out of its container and slice using a sharp knife. The slices may be cut into smaller portions. Try to use a straight-sided container so that the cheese can slide out easily.

1 Place the cherries in a large pan with the cinnamon sticks. Pour in enough water to almost cover the fruit. Bring to the boil, then cover and simmer for 20–30 minutes, or until the cherries are very tender. Remove the cinnamon sticks from the pan and discard.

2 Tip the fruit into a sieve and press into a bowl, using the back of a spoon. Measure the purée into a large, heavy pan, adding 350g/12oz/1¾ cups warmed sugar for every 600ml/1 pint/2½ cups purée.

3 Gently heat the purée, stirring, until the sugar dissolves. Increase the heat and cook for 45 minutes, stirring frequently, until very thick. To test, spoon a little of the cheese on to a cold plate; it should form a firm jelly.

4 Spoon into warmed, sterilized jars or oiled moulds. Seal, label, and store in a cool, dark place.

82 • curds, butters and cheeses

blackberry and apple cheese

This rich, dark preserve has an incredibly intense flavour and fabulous colour. For a fragrant twist, add a few raspberries – or even strawberries – in place of some of the blackberries.

Makes about 900g/2lb

INGREDIENTS

900g/2lb/8 cups blackberries

450g/1lb tart cooking apples, cut into chunks, with skins and cores intact

grated rind and juice of 1 lemon

800g/1¾lb/4 cups granulated sugar, warmed

1 Put the blackberries, apples and lemon rind and juice in a pan and pour in enough water to come halfway up the fruit. Bring to the boil, then uncover and simmer for 15–20 minutes or until the fruit is very soft.

2 Leave the fruit to cool slightly, then tip the mixture into a sieve and press into a bowl, using the back of a spoon. Measure the purée into a large, heavy pan, adding 400g/14oz/2 cups warmed sugar for every 600ml/1 pint/2½ cups purée.

3 Gently heat the purée, stirring, until the sugar dissolves. Increase the heat slightly and cook for 40–50 minutes, stirring frequently, until very thick (see Cook's Tip).

4 Spoon the blackberry and apple cheese into warmed, sterilized straight-sided jars or oiled moulds. Seal and label the jars or moulds, then store in a cool, dark place for 2–3 months to dry out slightly.

COOK'S TIP

When the cheese is ready, you should be able to see the base of the pan when a wooden spoon is drawn through the mixture. Spoon a small amount of the mixture on to a chilled plate; it should form a firm jelly.

sweet fruit preserves

Seasonal fruits bottled in spirits or syrups look stunning stacked in your store cupboard and taste divine spooned over ice cream, cakes and desserts. Some fruits can even be enjoyed on their own with just a spoonful of cream. Preserving in syrups and alcohol helps to retain the colour, texture and flavour of the fruit, while ensuring that it does not ferment or spoil on keeping. Alcohol also adds extra flavour and body and can turn simple preserved fruits into an indulgent treat.

mulled pears

These pretty pears in a warming spiced syrup make a tempting dessert, particularly during the cold winter months. Serve them with crème fraîche or vanilla ice cream, or in open tarts.

Makes about 1.3kg/3lb

INGREDIENTS

1.8kg/4lb small firm pears
1 orange
1 lemon
2 cinnamon sticks, halved
12 whole cloves
5cm/2in piece fresh root ginger, peeled and sliced
300g/11oz/1½ cups granulated sugar
1 bottle fruity light red wine

COOK'S TIP

Pears have a delicate flavour, so use a light, fruity wine such as Beaujolais or Merlot to make the syrup.

1 Peel the pears leaving the stalks intact. Peel very thin strips of rind from the orange and lemon, using a vegetable peeler. Pack the pears and citrus rind into large sterilized preserving jars, dividing the spices evenly between the jars.

2 Preheat the oven to 120°C/250°F/Gas ½. Put the sugar and wine in a large pan and heat gently, stirring, until the sugar has completely dissolved. Bring the mixture to the boil, then cook for 5 minutes.

3 Pour the wine syrup over the pears, making sure that there are no air pockets and that the fruits are completely covered with the syrup.

4 Cover the jars with their lids, but do not seal. Place them in the oven and cook for 2½–3 hours.

5 Carefully remove the jars from the oven, place on a dry dishtowel and seal. Leave the jars to cool completely, then label and store in a cool, dark place.

COOK'S TIP

To check that jars are properly sealed, leave them to cool for 24 hours, then loosen the clasp. Very carefully, try lifting the jar by the lid alone: if the jar is sealed properly, the lid should be fixed firmly enough to take the weight of the pot. Replace the clasp and store until ready to use.

poached spiced plums in brandy

Bottling plums in a spicy syrup is a great way to preserve the flavours of autumn and provide a store of instant desserts during the winter months. Serve them with whipped cream.

Makes about 900g/2lb

INGREDIENTS

600ml/1 pint/2½ cups brandy

rind of 1 lemon, peeled in a long strip

350g/12oz/1¾ cups caster (superfine) sugar

1 cinnamon stick

900g/2lb plums

VARIATION

Any member of the plum family can be preserved using this recipe. Try bottling damsons or wild yellow plums as a delicious alternative. Cherries will also work very well.

1 Put the brandy, lemon rind, sugar and cinnamon in a large pan and heat gently until the sugar dissolves. Add the plums and poach for 15 minutes until soft. Remove the fruit and pack in sterilized jars.

2 Boil the syrup rapidly until reduced by a third, then strain over the plums to cover. Seal the jars tightly. Label when cold and store for up to 6 months in a cool, dark place.

sweet fruit preserves • 87

peaches in peach schnapps

The fragrant taste of peaches is complemented and intensified by the addition of the schnapps. Serve with whipped cream flavoured with some of the syrup and a squeeze of lemon juice.

Makes about 1.3kg/3lb

INGREDIENTS

1.3kg/3lb firm peaches
1 litre/1¾ pints/4 cups water
900g/2lb/4½ cups granulated sugar
8 green cardamom pods
50g/2oz/½ cup whole blanched almonds, toasted
120ml/4fl oz/½ cup peach schnapps

VARIATION

Amaretto, an Italian liqueur flavoured with almond and apricot kernels, can be used instead of peach schnapps.

1 Put the peaches in a bowl and pour over boiling water. Drain immediately and peel, then halve and remove the stones (pits).

2 Put the water and half the sugar in a large pan and heat gently until the sugar has dissolved. Increase the heat and boil for 5 minutes.

3 Add the peaches to the syrup and return to the boil. Reduce the heat, cover and simmer gently for 5–10 minutes, or until tender but not too soft. Using a slotted spoon, remove the peaches and set aside to drain.

4 Put the cardamom pods and almonds in a large pan, then add 900ml/1½ pints/3¾ cups of the syrup and the remaining sugar.

5 Gently heat the syrup, stirring until the sugar has dissolved. Bring to the boil and boil until the syrup reaches 104°C/219°F. Leave to cool slightly, remove the cardamom pods, then stir in the schnapps.

6 Pack the peaches loosely in warmed sterilized jars. Pour the syrup and almonds over the fruit, twisting and gently tapping the jars to release any air bubbles. Seal and store in a cool, dark place for 2 weeks before eating.

pineapple in coconut rum

The tropical flavour of pineapple is enhanced by the addition of coconut rum. For a really special treat, serve topped with whipped cream and grated bitter chocolate.

3 Add the remaining sugar to the syrup and heat, stirring, until the sugar has dissolved completely. Bring to the boil and boil for about 10 minutes, or until the syrup has thickened. Remove from the heat and set aside to cool slightly, then stir in the coconut rum.

4 Pack the drained pineapple loosely in warmed sterilized jars. Pour in the syrup until the fruit is covered, tapping and twisting the jars to release any air bubbles. Seal, label and store in a cool, dark place for 2 weeks before eating.

COOK'S TIP
Choose plump pineapples that feel heavy for their size, with fresh, stiff plumes. To test for ripeness, gently pull out one of the bottom leaves; it should come out easily.

Makes about 900g/2lb

INGREDIENTS
- 1 orange
- 1.2 litres/2 pints/5 cups water
- 900g/2lb/4½ cups granulated sugar
- 2 pineapples, peeled, cored and cut into small chunks
- 300ml/½ pint/1¼ cups coconut rum

1 Thinly pare strips of rind from the orange, then slice into thin matchsticks. Put the water and half the sugar in a large pan with the orange rind and heat gently until the sugar has dissolved. Increase the heat and boil for 5 minutes.

2 Carefully add the pineapple pieces to the syrup and return to the boil. Reduce the heat and simmer gently for 10 minutes. Using a slotted spoon, remove the pineapple from the pan and set aside to drain.

sweet fruit preserves • 91

forest berries in Kirsch

This preserve captures the essence of the season in its rich, dark colour and flavour. Adding the sweet cherry liqueur Kirsch to the syrup intensifies the flavour of the bottled fruit.

Makes about 1.3kg/3lb

INGREDIENTS

1.3kg/3lb/12 cups mixed prepared summer berries, such as blackberries, raspberries, strawberries, redcurrants and cherries

225g/8oz/generous 1 cup granulated sugar

600ml/1 pint/2½ cups water

120ml/4fl oz/½ cup Kirsch

COOK'S TIP
Be careful not to overcook the fruits because they will lose their beautiful colour and fresh flavour.

1 Preheat the oven to 120°C/250°F/Gas ½. Pack the prepared fruit loosely into sterilized jars. Cover without sealing and place in the oven for 50–60 minutes, or until the juices start to run.

2 Meanwhile, put the sugar and water in a large pan and heat gently, stirring, until the sugar has dissolved. Increase the heat, bring to the boil and boil for 5 minutes. Stir in the Kirsch and set aside.

3 Carefully remove the jars from the oven and place on a dishtowel. Use the fruit from one of the jars to top up the rest.

4 Pour the boiling syrup into each jar, twisting and tapping each one to ensure that no air bubbles have been trapped. Seal, then store in a cool, dark place.

cherries in eau de vie

These potent cherries should be consumed with respect as they pack quite an alcoholic punch. Serve them with rich, dark chocolate torte or as a wicked topping for creamy rice pudding.

2 Spoon the sugar over the fruit, then pour in the eau de vie to cover and seal tightly.

3 Store for at least 1 month before serving, shaking the bottle now and then to help dissolve the sugar.

COOK'S TIP
Eau de vie actually refers to all spirits distilled from fermented fruits. Eau de vie is always colourless, with a high alcohol content (sometimes 45% ABV) and a clean, pure scent and the flavour of the founding fruit. Popular eaux de vie are made from cherries and strawberries.

Makes about 1.3kg/3lb

INGREDIENTS
450g/1lb/generous 3 cups ripe cherries
8 blanched almonds
75g/3oz/6 tbsp granulated sugar
500ml/17fl oz/scant 2¼ cups eau de vie

VARIATIONS
Strawberries, raspberries and blackcurrants are all excellent preserved in eau de vie. They will all produce fine fruity liqueurs as well as the macerated fruit.

1 Wash and stone (pit) the cherries then pack them into a sterilized, wide-necked bottle along with the blanched almonds.

sweet fruit preserves • 93

rumtopf

This fruit preserve originated in Germany, where special earthenware rumtopf pots are traditionally filled with fruits as they come into season. It is not necessary to use the specific pot; you can use a large preserving jar instead. Store in a cool, dark place.

Makes about 3 litres/5 pints/12½ cups

INGREDIENTS

900g/2lb fruit, such as strawberries, blackberries, blackcurrants, redcurrants, peaches, apricots, cherries and plums
250g/9oz/1¼ cups granulated sugar
1 litre/1¾ pints/4 cups white rum

1 Prepare the fruit: remove stems, skins, cores and stones (pits) and cut larger fruit into bitesize pieces. Combine the fruit and sugar in a large non-metallic bowl, cover and leave to stand for 30 minutes.

2 Spoon the fruit and juices into a sterilized 3 litre/5 pint/12½ cup preserving or earthenware jar and pour in the white rum to cover.

3 Cover the jar with clear film (plastic wrap), then seal and store in a cool, dark place.

4 As space allows, and as different fruits come into season, add more fruit, sugar and rum in appropriate proportions, as described above.

5 When the jar is full, store in a cool, dark place for 2 months. Serve the fruit spooned over ice cream or other desserts and enjoy the rum in glasses as a liqueur.

spiced apple mincemeat

This fruity mincemeat is traditionally used to fill little pies at Christmas but it is great at any time. Try it as a filling for large tarts finished with a lattice top and served with custard. To make a lighter mincemeat, add some extra grated apple just before using.

Makes about 1.8kg/4lb

INGREDIENTS

500g/1¼lb tart cooking apples, peeled, cored and finely diced

115g/4oz/½ cup ready-to-eat dried apricots, coarsely chopped

900g/2lb/5⅓ cups luxury dried mixed fruit

115g/4oz/1 cup whole blanched almonds, chopped

175g/6oz/1 cup shredded beef or vegetarian suet (chilled, grated shortening)

225g/8oz/generous 1 cup dark muscovado (molasses) sugar

grated rind and juice of 1 orange

grated rind and juice of 1 lemon

5ml/1 tsp ground cinnamon

2.5ml/½ tsp grated nutmeg

2.5ml/½ tsp ground ginger

120ml/4fl oz/½ cup brandy

1 Put the apples, apricots, dried fruit, almonds, suet and sugar in a large non-metallic bowl and stir together until thoroughly combined.

2 Add the orange and lemon rind and juice, cinnamon, nutmeg, ginger and brandy and mix well. Cover the bowl with a clean dishtowel and leave to stand in a cool place for 2 days, stirring occasionally.

3 Spoon the mincemeat into cool sterilized jars, pressing down well, and being very careful not to trap any air bubbles. Cover and seal.

4 Store the jars in a cool, dark place for at least 4 weeks before using. Once opened, store in the refrigerator and use within 4 weeks. Unopened, the mincemeat will keep for 1 year.

COOK'S TIP

If, when opened, the mincemeat seems dry, pour a little extra brandy or orange juice into the jar and gently stir in. You may need to remove a spoonful or two of the mincemeat from the jar to do this.

INDEX

alcohol 85
  apricots in amaretto syrup 88
  cherries in eau de vie 93
  clementine and liqueur marmalade 67
  forest berries in Kirsch 92
  mulled pears 86
  nectarines in brandy syrup 29
  peach and amaretto jam 39
  peaches in peach schnapps 90
  pineapple in coconut rum 91
  poached spiced plums in brandy 87
  preserving fruits in alcohol 29
  rumtopf 29, 94
  spiced cider and apple jelly 53
almond and greengage jam 42
apples: apple and cinnamon butter 76
  blackberry and apple cheese 83
  cranberry and apple cheese 23
  dried apple rings 28
  rosehip and apple jelly 52
  spiced apple mincemeat 95
  spiced cider and apple jelly 53
apricots: apricot and orange marmalade 68–9
  apricot butter 22–3
  apricots in amaretto syrup 88
  dried apricot jam 38

berries 33
  forest berries in Kirsch 92
blackberry and apple cheese 83
blackcurrant jam 37
blueberry and lime jam 36
bottled fruits 26–7
  fresh fruit salad 24
bottles 8–9
  sterilizing 10–11
butters 22, 71
  storage 11

candied fruit 26–7
candied peel 27
cardamoms: mango and cardamom butter 79
  red plum and cardamom jelly 49
cheesecloth 8
cheeses 23, 71
  storage 11
cherries: cherries in eau de vie 93
  cherry jam 14
  spiced cherry cheese 82
  summer fruit jam 13
cinnamon: apple and cinnamon butter 76
citrus fruits, peeling 21

clementine and liqueur marmalade 67
conserves 15, 33
  flavouring 15
containers 8, 10
cranberries: cranberry and apple cheese 23
  cranberry jelly 48
  pink grapefruit and cranberry marmalade 62
curds 22, 71
  storage 11
currants
  blackcurrant jam 37
  redcurrant jelly 16–17
  summer fruit jam 13

damson and vanilla cheese 80–1
damson jam 40–1
dishwashers 10
dried fruits 28
  dried apple rings 28
  dried apricot jam 38

equipment 8–9

figs infused with Earl Grey 89
flowers: gooseberry and elderflower jam 40–1
  scented geranium and pear jelly 55
  wild strawberry and rose petal conserve 35
forest berries in Kirsch 92
fruit: boiling twice 18
  fresh fruit salad 26
  frozen fruit 25
  fruit preserves 85
  leftover pulp 23
  pectin content 14
  stone fruits 33
funnels 9

ginger: lemon and ginger marmalade 64–5
  rhubarb and ginger jam 43
glacé fruit 27
gooseberries: gooseberry and elderflower jam 40–1
  red gooseberry jelly 50–1
  summer fruit jam 13
grapefruits: grapefruit curd 74
  pink grapefruit and cranberry marmalade 62
  ruby red grapefruit marmalade 63
greengage and almond jam 42
grenadine and pomegranate jelly 57

heat treatment 25
hedgerow fruits 33
  hedgerow jelly 46
herbs: rhubarb and mint jelly 50–1
hips: rosehip and apple jelly 52
hydrometer 9

jams 12–13, 33
  top tips 15
jars 8–9
  filling 11
  sterilizing 10–11
jellies 16, 45

flavouring 18
top tips 18
jelly bags 8, 17

kumquats: peach and kumquat marmalade 68–9

lemons: lemon and ginger marmalade 64–5
  lemon curd 30, 72
  microwave lemon curd 24
limes: blueberry and lime jam 36
  lime curd 22

mango and cardamom butter 79
marmalades 19, 59
  top tips 21
microwaves 11
  lemon curd 30
mincemeat, spiced apple 95
mint: rhubarb and mint jelly 50–1
mulberry jelly 47
mulled pears 86
muslin (cheesecloth) 8

nectarines in brandy syrup 29

oranges 59
  apricot and orange marmalade 68–9
  orange and coriander marmalade 64–5
  orange jelly marmalade 20–1
  pressure cooker orange marmalade 30–1
  St Clement's marmalade 61
  Seville orange curd 73
  Seville orange marmalade 19–20
Oxford marmalade 60

passion fruits: passion fruit curd 75
  pineapple and passion fruit jelly 56
  seedless raspberry and passion fruit jam 34
peaches: peach and amaretto jam 39
  peach and kumquat marmalade 68–9
  peaches in peach schnapps 90
pears: mulled pears 86
  pear and vanilla butter 77
  poached pears 24
  scented geranium and pear jelly 55
pectin 12, 14
pineapples: pineapple and passion fruit jelly 56
  pineapple in coconut rum 91
pink grapefruit and cranberry marmalade 62
plums: poached spiced plums in brandy 87
  red plum and cardamom jelly 49
pomegranate and grenadine jelly 57
preserving 6–7
  covering 9, 11
  equipment 8–9
  freezers 31
  microwaves 11, 30
  potting 10–11
  preserving fruits in alcohol 29

pressure cookers 25, 30–1
  orange marmalade 30–1–5
pumpkins: pumpkin and maple butter 78
  spiced pumpkin marmalade 66

quinces: quince and coriander jelly 54
  quince cheese 80–1

raspberries: seedless raspberry and passion fruit jam 34
  seedless raspberry jam 14
  summer fruit jam 13
red gooseberry jelly 50–1
red plum and cardamom jelly 49
redcurrant jelly 16–17
rhubarb: rhubarb and ginger jam 43
  rhubarb and mint jelly 50–1
rosehip and apple jelly 52
ruby red grapefruit marmalade 63
rumtopf 29, 94

St Clement's marmalade 61
scented geranium and pear jelly 55
seedless raspberry and passion fruit jam 34
seedless raspberry jam 14
setting 12
Seville orange curd 73
Seville orange marmalade 19–20
spreads 13
sterilizing containers 10–11
stone fruits 33
storage 11
strawberries:
  strawberry conserve 15
  strawberry freezer jam 31
  summer fruit jam 13
  wild strawberry and rose petal conserve 35
sugar: reduced-sugar preserves 11, 31
  sugar syrups 26
sugar thermometers 8
summer fruit jam 13
syrups 24, 29, 85, 88

testing for setting 12
top tips 15, 18, 21

vanilla: damson and vanilla cheese 80–1
  pear and vanilla butter 77

wild strawberry and rose petal conserve 35